Music Soothes the Soul

Matthew Bernstein

WALDORF PUBLISHING

Published by Waldorf Publishing
2140 Hall Johnson Road
#102-345
Grapevine, Texas 76051
www.WaldorfPublishing.com

Music Soothes the Soul

ISBN: 9781634432627
Library of Congress Control Number: 2014958725

Printed in the United States of America

Front cover photo credit: Brett Ryder

Dedication

This book is dedicated to Honey and Poppee, my grandparents, who have been there every step of the way. Thank you for believing in me, for your endless support, for inspiring me, and for sharing everything in my life. I love you.

Disclaimer

The author and publisher have made every effort to be 100% accurate with all of the interviews and conversations that the author had while creating this book.

The author and publisher are making every effort to ensure that the information in this book was correct at press time. The author and publisher do not assume and hereby disclaim any liability to any party for any loss, damage, or disruption caused by errors or omissions, whether such errors or omissions result from negligence, accident, or any other cause.

Table of Contents

Foreword by Larry Thomas
founder of the Fender Music Foundation

Music is a powerful force. The benefits of music run as deep as one's soul, and it has always taken me to a special place. I've been fortunate to spend my life around music, with musicians, instrument-makers, and the blessings of blending a deep passion with a daily job. As a teenager, I learned to play the guitar, and, throughout my life, musical instruments and the sounds they make have fascinated me.

During the last few years of working as CEO of Guitar Center Inc., I became aware of the battles of school districts around the country fighting to keep music and the arts a part of a daily curriculum for kids. Once I retired, I founded the Guitar Center Music Foundation in 2005, as a way to give back to the industry and life that has been so great to me. We started in a small office with a Rolodex and hopes of spreading the joy of music-making. In 2010, when I joined Fender as the CEO, we changed the name to the Fender Music Foundation.

I think one of the things that make the Foundation unique is that we have always had a national view; we're not just trying to build our school programs locally in Southern California. Although we are called the Fender Music Foundation, our donations come from many like-minded folks around the country; artists, music enthusiasts, charity-minded people, and manufacturers. The foundation is about the people who serve, and the programs to which we donate. Our grants have been delivered across many of the states in the country. It has been especially rewarding to read letters and see videos from donations to cancer centers, prisons, children's hospitals, small music programs, and Indian reservations, as

1

well as after-school programs like the Boys and Girls Club. Many of our grants are to the small programs under the 'radar' of large foundations.

Music matters. It is part of the fabric of our culture and an essential part of our lives. *Music Soothes the Soul* is a must-read for anyone who loves music. Matthew Bernstein, at the age of 17, has interviewed 70 fascinating music leaders from many countries who share a common passion, which is their love of music. In writing this book, Matthew's goals were to inspire his readers and provide opportunities for children to imagine, create, and express themselves through music. All proceeds from book sales are being donated to the Fender Music Foundation to keep music programs healthy and vibrant across the nation. Music makes a difference in the world, in tangible and intangible ways. Every story shows why music is empowering and powerful, and how it positively can benefit us all.

Introduction

Music was a fundamental feature in our home. An eclectic mix of dad's rock and roll, mom's country, my little brother's Putumayo World Music, and The Wiggles, kept me company. A drawer in our kitchen cabinet was labeled "Matthew's Music Box". I remember pulling the chrome handle to find shiny pots, metal cups, and plastic bowls waiting for me. All I needed to do was bang these containers together, and they were instantly transformed into my own musical instruments. As I grew, my musical knowledge and experience expanded. I've played cello in the classical orchestra, and electric guitar in the jazz orchestra. I currently sing in three different symphonic choirs. Music makes me feel happy. It is my way of communicating.

My parents tell me this love of music comes naturally. They enjoy sharing the family story about how my great-grandfather met my great-grandmother. He was an avid scientist who loved to tinker and experiment. His mother's kitchen was the perfect laboratory. They loved to listen to the radio while she cooked and he tinkered. One day Gramps put his ear closer to the radio to hopefully hear who had sung that moving song. On the other end of the airwaves, my great-grandmother had her debut. When they later met, he told her it was love at the very first note. Music changed their lives.

I was 11 when the retirement home across the street from my school asked if any musicians wanted to play for the residents. I jumped at the chance to perform. With my red Fender electric guitar slung over my back and 30 rock songs memorized, I felt ready on show day. Entering the large room, I saw residents sitting in wheelchairs or holding onto walkers. Anxiety began to rumble in my stomach as I wondered if my rock-song theme was the right choice. I got to the small stage and, after a quick introduction, started with "Yellow Submarine". The moment my hand strummed the strings, the audience woke up as if electrified. I heard hands clapping and saw feet tapping as I rolled through the chorus. "Sing it louder, sing it again!" voices instructed me. I must have sung that song six times and, with each round, more voices accompanied me. We moved through many Beatles' tunes. Downcast eyes and sagging heads were transformed to smiling faces. As the performance came to an end, I heard a voice from the back ask if I knew any Jay-Z because it was one of his grandson's favorite artists. To my surprise, voices all joined in on the chorus of "Holy Grail". That was the day I learned how powerful music can be.

Music Soothes the Soul developed from my musical experiences. Knowing how music can be transformative, I wanted to hear and share other people's connection to music. I started my adventure by writing a weekly column for *Oregon Music News* called "Music on the Street". My goal was to explore a variety of personal musical stories. Each week I interviewed someone who had a story to share: the inventor who turned garbage cans and torn Home Depot bags into instruments, the nonprofit executive who took guitars into youth detention centers, the celebrity who learned to speak English from listening to rock and roll. *Music Soothes the Soul* shares my journey. Inside these pages are the personal narratives of 70 amazing artists, musicians, scientists, teachers, and entrepreneurs who embraced music and changed their lives. Travel with me to Europe and Canada, and across the United States. Discover what I've found to be true; although we come from different places, music is our universal language. Let's celebrate our connections.

Prepare to be inspired.

Chapter One: Art Alexakis

Matthew Bernstein

Art Alexakis was raised in the projects of Mar Vista Gardens by a single mother. Music provided solace for the losses in his life: his brother died of a heroin overdose, his teenage girlfriend committed suicide, his father left home. In 1992, Art formed Everclear, an alt-rock band that would go on to have three platinum albums. Art was named Modern Rock Artist of the Year by *Billboard Magazine* in 1998, but has also found personal growth as an actor, activist, and most of all a father.

"Growing up was really hard. I had a tough life. I came from a broken home. My dad left when I was five. We were so poor we had to move into a housing project near Culver City in California. The one constant for me was music. I grew up in the 1960s when rock 'n' roll and The Beatles were taking over the world. Every boy who couldn't play football was playing guitar in his garage. I just fell in love with rock 'n' roll from the earliest time that I can remember. My letter to Santa when I was four years old asked for an electric guitar, an organ, a drum set, the whole nine yards. I wanted it all. I can truly say that I never wanted to do anything else but play music."

"While I hoped Everclear would be a success I never imagined it would become what it has. I was living in Portland at the time and I had a baby on the way. I was on welfare when my daughter was born to pay for the hospital bills and working minimal wage jobs so I could do my music at night. I had been playing in bands my whole life so I thought I'd start a band there. I put an ad in the personals of the local music paper, *The Rocket*, and I found a bass player and a drummer. We became a popular Portland band and when we went to make our first record called "World of Noise*"* I could barely find the money. I remember it cost $400 and I worked a trade of some stuff I had."

"It was a tough time. My life was skewed towards being a father because of my own childhood experience. But I knew that rather than give up the dream I just had to work all the harder for it in order to provide a better life. I knew that if I wasn't happy and fulfilled then I wouldn't be a good dad. I would be like my mom and other parents I knew who weren't doing what they wanted to do. I wanted to be the best parent but I also wanted more as a parent and that was to be a musician. That's why I think people need to do what they love to do. It has to be genuine."

"I love what I do. I get to play guitar in a rock band and I make a decent living, so I feel like I'm living the dream. I get to be creative. I put my ideas, my art, my dreams, and my soul into what I do every day. I perform on stage and it feels good when I finish a song and people clap. Do I do it for that? Not really, but it is something I like. Do I do it for the money? Not really, but I like money. I do it because I am not really good at anything else and that is why I think people should do what they like because that usually turns out to be the right thing."

"I've come to realize over the years that with creative things like music it either comes or it doesn't. You can't fake it. You can't teach somebody to be creative. You can teach them the craft of songwriting. You can teach them the skills of songwriting or what it's like being in a band or being a musician but to teach someone how to emote is impossible. My inspiration comes from my life, from other people's lives, from the things I read, see, and think about. My inspiration is everywhere. When I feel it I write down the words or talk them into my phone."

"I think that what a person ultimately does matters less than what type of person they are. I try to be a good guy and be present. I am aware and sober and work really hard to be a better person. If I make a mistake, I try

7

to fix it. Good people do bad things but I make reparations when necessary. That's the main thing: I just try to do the best I can at everything I do. I try to put myself in wholeheartedly. It wasn't something I did when I was younger."

"Music matters to me because . . . making music is the closest I ever get to the real me. It's the best way I have found of expressing to the world who I am."

Chapter Two: Adam Banton

Photo Credit: Erik Hilburn

Adam Banton is considered one of seven Odyssey Legends. A sponsored rider who started in 1987 at the young age of 13, Adam is also a professional musician who has been a featured athlete on Daily Habit. His creative and energetic music has been a part of BMX videos for over 10 years.

"Everything music-related had to do with BMX when I was a kid. I started riding seriously when I was 13. My only input for music was whatever bands were being played in the BMX videos I watched constantly. Those were the bands that inspired me to go to the record store the very next day after I saw them, and buy their album. It just so happened at the time that these bands were hardcore punk. I grew up in Northern Virginia, so many were local hero bands."

"I went to a really small high school, and they didn't offer much. I was riding my bike and ditching classes to go to contests. There was a passion there that I had, but I didn't really have an outlet to plug into through the educational system. My dad bought me my first guitar and I really wanted to take a class. My last year, senior year, the school offered a music class, and it was with everybody jumbled together who wanted to play some type of instrument. You had the percussion dudes, maybe one bass player, and there was a very small handful of us guitar players. It was cool that they offered the class, but it didn't influence me to become a musician. It wasn't structured to give me the skills so, when I graduated from high school, I left wanting to play an instrument."

"The one event that made me want to be a guitar player was that I broke my leg and my ankle really badly riding my bike, and I ended up having to drop out of community college in Richmond, Virginia. I had to move back home. I remember there were three different doctors huddling in the emergency room, talking about possible amputation. This was in North Carolina. They called my parents in Virginia, and they told my dad the situation. My dad said 'No, whatever you do, do not amputate his foot.'"

"It's all kind of a blur to me, but for almost a year I was healing from that broken leg. They didn't amputate. They didn't even have to do surgery, actually, which was great. But that's also why it took such a long time to heal. Through those 11 months, I got out that acoustic guitar my dad had bought me. Since I was stuck in a bed, I would keep my guitar beside the bed and start strumming."

"When I got better, they bought me a used Fender Stratocaster, which I totally fell in love with. After that injury, that was really the big turning point for me: having all that downtime to play music. It was the first time I was taken away 100% from my bike. I had nothing to focus on, and I just put all my energy into playing guitar and making music. For the first time in my life, that was when I really felt that I liked something just as much as riding my bike. If I am not on my bike or on a bike trip, then I am most likely at home playing my guitar. I don't know why, but I've always felt like it's hard for me to focus on only one of these life passions. They are my two sides."

"My music is instrumental. When I'm riding my bike, it has to be the hardcore music to psyche me up. That's a part of me. When I relax, I listen to chill music. These two sides influence my music. I find my inspiration in life's experiences; good experiences, bad experiences. I try to create music that triggers memories or feelings or hopes for the future. If the listeners can bring my music along with them on their journey and feel inspired by it, I can't ask for any more than that. I think that's why I call my latest album 'Escapism'. I've been working on it for about six years. That name was one of the most natural and easiest parts of the process. It was loud and clear when it came to me, and felt 100% right."

"Music matters to me because . . . it expresses every type of emotion that a human can feel."

Chapter Three: Jessica Baron

Jessica Baron devotes herself to music and cannot remember a time when music was not a focal point in her life. Trained as a music educator, child-development specialist, and counselor, she shares her passion for music in as many ways as she can think of. She began her teaching career at 12 and has since worked as a full-time music teacher in a variety of schools. Jessica has authored seven books all related to music instruction, including the successful Music Makers curriculum for the Boys and Girls Clubs of America, as well as the International House of Blue's Foundation's Make an Impression guitar program. Her best-selling guitar method, SmartStart Guitar, is based on the idea that making music is essentially a hands-on, creative, and auditory process that should be fun and stress-free. She also works as a guitar instructor online, for jamplay.com. But perhaps her most significant contribution to the world of music comes with founding the nonprofit, Guitars in the Classroom, in 1998, to train and equip classroom teachers in order to integrate singing and playing guitar and ukulele into the daily school experience. The program has grown to serve over 30 states and parts of Canada, positively impacting the lives of more than 800,000 students.

"My family loved music, and therefore I loved music from the time I was little. We had a piano in the house, and my father would play it constantly. My mother loved folk music and made a point of playing folk recordings for us. They also brought my brother and me to hear Ella Jenkins and Pete Seeger when we were little. For me, the die was cast with those early experiences. I started guitar lessons when I was seven, and was immediately taken with the instrument. I started teaching other people how to play guitar when I was 12. Over the years, I trained as a music educator, child-development specialist, and counselor, and worked in schools in the Los Angeles area, and Santa Cruz, California, teaching music."

"What inspired me to start Guitars in the Classroom was when I noticed that the subject teachers wanted to be able to connect with their students in the same way that I connected with kids through the arts. They wanted to have that same high energy and engagement in the classroom that students were experiencing in music class. A number of the teachers shared that they had always wanted to learn to make music, so I started thinking about how to empower them to incorporate music into daily classroom subjects. I saw how music transformed my own students. It provided an outlet for their feelings, and an inroad to explore those feelings as well as a colorful palette with which to paint lesson content and big ideas. With some sponsorship, experimentation, and encouragement from like-minded people, Guitars in the Classroom became a reality in 1998."

"Guitars in the Classroom does so much good. It's a life-changer for teachers who want to be more creative in their lives and work. They come together, connect, learn to make, lead, and compose music, and invent ways to interweave music with general learning across the academic curriculum. Then they make it a life-changer for children. We've trained over 9,000 teachers. For most of the teachers, it's something they've never tried before. Music is an exciting journey. There are so many ways we are discovering together to use music to help kids learn."

"Music helps by engaging all children and especially those who face challenges in school. For students who have difficulty learning in traditional ways or fitting in, and for those acquiring English as a second language, making music, singing, strumming, and songwriting can provide a powerful medium for understanding, connecting, memorizing, collaborating, and so much more. Music can make a critical difference, harnessing intuition, sparking inspiration, and carrying a positive mood

15

forward throughout the school day, while utilizing very specialized skills and talents. And with this medium, students can become a part of something bigger than themselves, something from which they can draw ability and to which they can contribute with their own creativity."

"Music matters to me because . . . it nurtures the individual and brings everyone together, no matter what language we speak."

Chapter Four: Jennifer Batten

There aren't many female rock guitarists. So how did a young woman from upstate New York get to be the lead guitarist for Michael Jackson and Jeff Beck – two legendary musicians in a male-dominated field? From an early age, Jennifer Batten had talent and drive. She refused to believe the stereotype that a woman couldn't cut it, and set out to prove herself. She has become a legend in her own right, with her two-handed tapping style, which allows her more speed and to combine chord clusters otherwise unreachable with only the left hand. Her unique style of blending blues, jazz, rock, and world music chronicles her dramatic journey to fame.

"In the town where I grew up, we used to have musicians stay at our house when they were traveling through on their tours. Music was always playing in the house. It was just part of the family culture. I was totally influenced by the Beatles as a kid. It made me want to take guitar lessons. At eight, I got my first guitar. It was a red and blue electric. I remember that when I turned 12, I announced to my mom that I wanted to be a guitarist. My parents supported my choice and I attended the Musician's Institute, where I learned most of my skills. I graduated in 1979. It was their third class ever. I got started on two-handed tapping, which became my signature style, from a fellow student, Steve Lynch."

"Being in the L.A. music scene, and around that environment all the time, helped me as I tried to get into bands. I was lucky enough to hear about the auditions for Michael Jackson from a Musicians Institute's referral service. Hearing about the auditions is usually the hardest part of getting in with a band. Usually big names like that will use people they have used before and you don't ever hear about it. It's a very tight clique, so it was a lucky break that he was doing open auditions. Michael wasn't there in person, which made it much more relaxing for everybody. I auditioned in front of a video camera, and he looked at videotapes of everyone's audition. I got a call a couple of days later and was told he was interested in me. Then it was a matter of going down and rehearsing with the band, to see how it went. It wasn't like I had the gig at that point. I still had to do more to prove myself to the musical director and Michael."

"I didn't meet Michael for another month after rehearsals began. His entire team worked on getting the whole show together, but we were always rehearsing in separate rooms. Sometimes we would rehearse for 10 or 12 hours a day. There was a room for dancers, one for the singers, and one for the band. After that initial month, I finally met him when we moved to rehearse on a big production stage. We spent about two months total getting ready. Everything had to be perfect. The rest is pretty much history. I got my passport processed and received a flight ticket to Tokyo, and we toured for a year and a half."

"I played with Michael for 10 years, from 1987 through 1997. I was his lead guitarist on Bad, Dangerous, and HIStory, and all three of his solo tours. The Super Bowl was very memorable because it was the largest television audience in history. It was really exciting because it was live, and whatever mistakes happened would be recorded forever. Knowing that really keeps you on your toes. For me, the most rewarding part of performing is the interaction I have with my fans."

"Music matters to me because . . . it's the soundtrack of our lives. Ever since the caveman started to beat out rhythm, it has been part of every culture on Earth. It's as important as language."

Chapter Five: Tim Bavington

Music sits at the center of Tim Bavington's paintings. As a young child in England, Tim spent hours immersed in art. Born in 1966, the musical world emerging from 1960s rock, and later punk rock, pulled him in. His art reflects both influences as he effectively blends art and sound. Tim has developed a system to attribute color to notes, which then allows him to artistically interpret songs. Famous tracks from groups such as The Rolling Stones and The Kingsmen are transformed into vibrant bands of bright colors. His works have appeared in the Museum of Modern Art, New York, The Museum of Contemporary Art, San Diego, and The Portland Art Museum, Portland, Oregon.

"My parents lived in London during the 1960s, the time rock 'n' roll was being introduced in England. They met at a club called Eel Pie Island, which was a jazz club in London. This club was the first club that had the Rolling Stones as a house band. My parents fell in love with the Stones and listened to them often before the band became famous. I was born right in the middle of these musical beginnings. When I entered high school, music was really changing in England. Punk rock was making a big impact, and that had its effect on me. The music that came out of the late 1970s really got my attention. I was very enthusiastic about music, but I think that's fairly common for any kid during that era."

"I found myself interested in abstract painting about 25 years ago. I was still in college and was training to be a commercial artist, because I wanted to get a job as an artist. Commercial art is usually meant for advertising. I was more interested in abstract painting, what many people call 'high–art', which is typically associated with museums or galleries. About 10 years ago, I started thinking about how I would name abstract paintings after songs that I liked. Many painters do that. I wanted to take pop music as a genre, which I feel is under-appreciated, and combine it with abstract art in some way. This would make my art accessible."

"I began this process by first looking at the sheet music for a song I like. Jimi Hendrix was an artist who broke the rules. I love and admire his work. The earliest painting that I did was the translation of a Hendrix's guitar solo. It's called 'Study for a Voodoo Child'. That piece hangs in the Portland Art Museum. The reason I chose a solo to do for my first painting was because the musical score was short. It was only 16 bars."

"I look at the scores and translate the piece of music to a canvas by assigning a color to each of the notes in the key of the music. The note becomes a stripe, and the width of that stripe is determined by the length the note is held. A long note would be a wide stripe; a short note would be a skinny stripe. Hendrix uses a lot of 16th notes and mini triplets which are almost impossible to transcribe. They make really skinny lines, and this inspires creativity for me. Hendrix gave me something that was unique. The musical pattern of Hendrix's guitar solo, when translated into the color blocks, creates a sort of psychedelic barcode painting."

"I really think it doesn't matter if you become a mathematician or an accountant or a businessman; the only way to survive, the only way that you will stand out, is by using your creativity. Creativity inspires. It is something that we use in everyday life. If you don't create, you will be beaten by the competition. Creativity is not given enough importance. If you learn to think creatively, you have something you can use wherever you go. Learning creativity through music or art, or whatever a school might teach, can be carried with you for the rest of your life. This is why it should be given much more importance."

"Music matters to me because . . . without music, life would not be as rich as it is. In addition to that, music is essential to the identity of the culture, as it is a popular way for people to express themselves."

Chapter Six: Dave Benning

Dave Benning's journey always begins with a photograph and ends with a portrait that captures his subject's musical soul. Dave grew up in England, in a home shared by music and art. His older siblings blared the Beatles, the Rolling Stones, and Jimi Hendrix. While Dave enjoyed the music playing off those vinyl records, it was the wildly colorful album covers that inspired him. Dave would spend hours creating intricate mock-ups of his own. This informal study led to a formal education in art and graphic design. Dave eventually set up shop in Vancouver, BC, and it would not be long before he would be known as Vancouver's premier celebrity portraitist.

"I start with a simple photographic image of the person I want to paint. But then I immerse myself in that person's history. If I was getting ready to paint Ringo Starr, for example, I'd listen to the Beatles music for a week or so before I even start on the painting. I'd watch the Beatles in concerts. I'd look at books and read biographies. I try to learn just as much about the person that I am painting as I possibly can. I want to tell that musical story in paint. I would even listen to the Beatles for the entire duration of the painting. If I was going to paint Jimi Hendrix, I'd follow exactly the same process."

"There is something very special that happens when I listen to the person's music while I am painting his or her portrait. The people I paint have life stories and music that others identify with, so I think that listening to that music while I am painting brings out that person's influence. I want my portraits to capture the spirit, fire, and spark of that life. I know when I have accomplished a good portrait, because it will actually capture that soul."

"I have painted lots of rock stars, like Alice Cooper, Buddy Guy, and the band Rush. Gene Simmons was really the first rock star that I met. Meeting the stars at the end is the real icing on the cake for me, because there are some musicians out there that you never get a chance to meet. Shaking their hand and showing them my artwork, which began from a tiny photograph, is just incredible. I feel very, very blessed being able to do this kind of thing."

"Before I painted rock stars, I was not a huge rock star fan. I knew the big hits and that was it. But now I know the rich history of the genre. When I learn about the musician's personal history and then meet that person, it's inspiring for me. My goal is to inspire others. If I can inspire a young kid to paint rock stars, it makes it all the more exciting for me. Art is very wide open, so you can do whatever you want. I think everyone should grab a paintbrush and have some fun. Creating something, whether in music or art, is definitely good for the soul."

"Music matters to me because . . . it gives life expression. Without music, the world would be very sad."

Chapter Seven: Eric Bieschke

The chief scientist for Pandora, the Internet's leading radio service, Eric Bieschke found music by listening. He also serves as the VP of Playlists. Using billions of musicological data points to deliver the perfect playlists seems simple now, but Eric was the one who derived the algorithms to do just that. Pandora has over 250 million users, who listen to over one billion hours of music per month. Using musical tastes to find ads that are more appealing is a unique job, but it fits both sides of Eric's interests perfectly.

"I grew up in a house with two sisters and a mother. My mother listened to New Age jazz for the most part, so this is the music my sisters and I grew up with. The very first music I bought was the Batman movie soundtrack from the movie with Michael Keaton. That soundtrack spoke to me. Probably my earliest connection to music was through movies on the soundtrack side, and then show tunes on the musical-theater side. I saw dozens of shows and musical theater growing up. My mom made me take piano lessons when I was 12. I did that for about a year. As I grew up, I shifted away from theater tunes and got more into club music and dancing. I think I always preferred being a music-listener. Dancing to music came later. I wasn't into the creation of music at all."

"What I do today came out of a combination of software engineering and my love of music. I was always into video games and computer games growing up, but I was not allowed to have a video game system. We weren't allowed to watch much TV either. I would have to go to a friend's house to play Nintendo. When I went to college at the University of Berkeley, I worked on computers and started programming. Working on the technical front with computers started my career in software engineering. I was a full-time student at Cal, and in March of 2000, I decided it would be a good idea to take a full-time job on top of my full-time educational career. I started tacking on video games and computer programming to those things I really love to do, and that took up all of my extra-curricular time. I interviewed with the founders of the company that was to become Pandora and they hired me."

"I began as a junior software developer. It just so happened I was now with a company that was doing all this music software creation. In 2005, Pandora became an online radio service. When we did that, my general software engineering became focused on writing software programs to connect people with the music they love. It's weird to think about now, but in 2005 it wasn't clear whether or not this online music would catch on, or whether Pandora would work. But it did. Since then, over the last nine years, my job has shifted from being a software engineer who was actually writing the code, to the person who builds teams of scientists, musicians, music curators, and software engineers. These teams have put their brains together to build all of the software systems that we have, in order for Pandora to create the individualized music playlists for people. I kept the musical side and the computer side of me and they morphed into something else. Being a music scientist combines all the things I love, all the time."

"We have a company culture at Pandora built around the 'Pandora Principles', which we use to help guide our thinking, decision-making, and the actions we take. One of the principles is: 'Advertising is our oxygen'. The way we think about advertising at Pandora is to use it to meet our primary goal. The primary goal is to connect everybody in the world with the music they love, but to make that happen it costs a lot of money. Advertising in this day and age allows us to do that."

"Over the last 13 years, we have done research about why people love music and how to connect people with that music. It turns out that the world of advertising is very similar. We looked at how we could apply the concepts of music personalization with ad customization. For every hour of listening to Pandora, we want to connect people with whatever products they connect with in their lives. If we do this well, we believe people will enjoy the listening experience more. For example, I am really into snowboarding, and I like going to clubs to go dancing. If I experience ads for those things, those are value ads. My life is better if I hear an ad for a snowboard that I am interested in or some cool dance party in San Francisco, which is where I live. We believe that by picking the type of advertising for people based on their musical interests, it is actually an enhancement to their lives."

"In terms of how we make that happen, there is a science to it. By listening to Pandora, people create lots and lots of data. The data on the music side helps us connect them with the music they love. We can look at the data for the millions and millions of people who have used Pandora and say, 'Hey look, this group of people likes this type of music'. We can then make inferences about that group. We predict how certain music is going to make them feel, or what political or cultural preferences they have. The same thing is true in advertising. With the data we have about what kind of things they click on, we can figure out what products they buy. Some of that data is then leveraged to make the music better for those people, and some is highly leveraged to connect people with the right type of advertising. They feed on each other. If you are playing the music they like and use an ad that fits with their data, then the disruption in their listening experience is much less. If the music is really good, they are in a better mood and more likely to respond to advertising. It is a great situation for Pandora to be in, where we can blend both sides of the equation to make the whole experience stronger."

"Music matters to me because . . . it makes life better."

Chapter Eight: Carla De Santis Black

Carla De Santis Black, is considered a leading advocate for women in rock music. She created ROCKRGRL magazine in 1994. It was the first national publication for female musicians in the United States. The popular magazine lasted for eleven years and, in its run, featured famous female artists of the time such as Joan Jett, Courtney Love, Tegan and Sara, and Tori Amos. The complete magazine series has been acquired by many renowned museums, libraries, and universities including The Smithsonian, Smith, Harvard, Cornell, and Duke, for their American Women's Historical artifacts collections. Carla continues to advocate for women's advancement in the music arena.

"I never knew a time when music was not playing in some way in our house. My parents were both pretty involved in music. They had a large record collection, and I would spend hours listening to the albums that I really loved on the hi-fi. My dad managed bands in Boston. He did a lot of public relations and played the music he represented. My mom taught piano when I was growing up, so there were always kids coming in and out of the house to take their piano lessons. Music was something that was always around."

"ROCKRGRL came out of my reaction to an article written in the mid-1990s. It was Rolling Stone Magazine's Women in Rock issue where they interviewed these women about their perfume, who they were dating, what they were wearing, but they never talked to them about their music. It really made me angry, because I had noticed in music magazines, when articles were written about women, they were usually done in a way that was demeaning. It seemed like people thought, 'Wow, you're a girl and you're talented,' or 'Wow, you're young and you write your own songs,' and that was it. The men were never treated that way. I wanted to create a place where women could talk about music. I wanted to read more about women as musicians rather than perfume-wearers. I wanted something where we could talk about what kind of instruments we played, or what kind of amps we used, or what strings we liked. So that is how the magazine began. Most of the women said it was the first time they were ever asked those types of questions."

"I decided to stop doing the magazine at the end of 2005. It was getting to be very apparent that people wanted instant information on the Web. The industry was going in a direction where the costs of printing were becoming really prohibitive. When I moved to Boston at the end of 2010, I wanted to do something that was 'ROCKRGRL-ish', but do it on the Web and do it in a slightly different way. I had this idea for MEOW, which was Musicians for Equal Opportunity for Women. When I came up with the acronym, it was just too good not to use. Basically it had the same mission as ROCKRGRL, but it was more Internet-based."

"I had the website for a year and a half. I updated it every day, with news about women in music, but also with the mission of talking about equality. Some of the questions I posed were: Why do we still talk about women as if they are third-class citizens in the music world when we have had so many great inspirational women? Why aren't we talking about the next great female guitar player? Why, when we're talking about shredders, are we talking about men for the most part? Or why, when we are talking about great drummers, is our first thought a man? Women are usually a second thought. I stopped doing it at the end of 2013 because, again, it was just so hard to finance. It was very difficult to get sponsorship and to get people in a room together, because they didn't want to spend the money. I think opportunities for enlightenment are certainly there, but not everybody picks up on them, even today."

"I am selling real estate, and all the people in my real estate group are either musicians, or people who have worked in the music industry, because we consider ourselves creative people. We understand how creative people think and the kinds of things that they want. I also coach musicians, especially female musicians, as far as goal-setting and coming up with ideas on how to make music work on their own terms. There were so many people along the way who gave me light-bulb moments. Now what inspires me are people who are doing what they want on their own terms, doing things in a different way and creating interesting ways to do those things. I like seeing people being true to themselves, no matter what that takes. I try to be one of those people and help others do the same."

"Music matters to me because . . . it brings people together in a way other things don't. You can listen to music and have a very individual experience, or you can be in a big crowd and have a shared experience. Music is something that crosses all boundaries."

Chapter Nine: Gene Bowen

Gene Bowen has seen music from all sides. As a child, he loved to listen to it and watch musicians perform. As an adult, he worked in the industry as tour manager for some of the biggest names in the business. He speaks frankly about his addiction and how he found the strength to quit. From that life transformation, he decided to help others, especially teens who had no one. He founded his nonprofit, Road Recovery, in 1998. It has helped over 50,000 young people battle addiction and other adversities. His organization uses the support of entertainment industry professionals who have had similar experiences, and professionals in the mental health field to empower young people to overcome.

"I came into music with no musical ability. I remember being a spectator of the magic that happens on stage, and feeling completely engulfed. The live music gave me a tremendous sense of peace. I was blown away. It became an unquenchable thirst, and I needed to be around music and see it. My parents would often say, 'You bought the record, why do you need to see the show?' I would say, 'You just don't understand. The record is powerful, but when I see it come to life on stage between the musicians, and see the energy that comes forth between the band and the audience, it's something divine'."

"I always had difficulty with transition and change. I struggled with that as a kid. But somehow or another, when I was in the presence of live music, all my fears and anxiety about life went away, and I would have this tremendous sense of peace, so I just chased that. It was my passion and my tenacity that got me into the music business."

"When I got older, I began to look beyond what was happening on the stage and saw there were people involved in making what happened on stage come to life and become a reality. I decided to explore that area of music and did so by asking questions. By the time I was in high school, I was going up early in the afternoon of shows to the backstage. I learned about what took place before the show to make it happen. I also realized that being in that gave me tranquility. One thing led to another and I started to make connections. I began with venues in the New York area. I spent the four years of high school just doing that, so by the time I had graduated and was in my tenure of high school, I had already made numerous connections. I was already getting offered jobs to go on the road."

"When I determined I had no musical ability, but I still had passion and drive to be around this magic, it led me to begin at the bottom with unloading trucks. Soon I discovered that I had logistical abilities, and I saw myself rise from unloading, to the organizational side. I then became a tour manager, spending the next 15 years on the road, touring with bands."

"I continued on this journey and this interesting career being a tour manager, but it is extremely unstable. You've got a gig and go from one tour to another, or if you are lucky enough to be with artists that tour then you have more employment; but things happen. Tours get canceled. People get sick or record companies decide not to continue to promote a record because there aren't that many hits on it. Things change, and that brings anxiety if you try to make a living that way. So for me, the underlying theme of my life was always fear. The way I handled those fears and those anxieties was through alcohol and drugs. When one drug didn't work well, I would switch to another one. I finally crossed that imaginary line. I became addicted and needed to use substances to survive. This led me to a downward spiral. My career disintegrated to the point where because of my dependence on drugs I could no longer maintain a job and the responsibilities of being a tour manager on the road."

"It got to the point where I was losing those jobs, and I ended up going back full circle to the beginning. I wound up working for the stage unions in New York and New Jersey, and was basically back to unloading trucks. I will never forget when the bands that I had worked with as a manager were playing those large venues. Of course they had not heard from me in a while and when they would come in to do a show they would see me unloading trucks. They would say, 'What are you doing? Why are you doing this?' and I would make up some excuse, but everybody knew that basically drugs had taken over my life. I could no longer hold onto those other management positions."

"I was very close to expiring. In 1992, I went into treatment for drug addiction and alcoholism. I got clean, and walked away from the music business."

"When an artist named Jeff Buckley, who was signed to Columbia Records, needed a tour manager, Jack Bookbinder, a manager and a friend I had worked with, remembered me, and called me up. At this point I had been clean for about two years. I ended up taking the job as tour manager for Jeff Buckley's world tour (1994-1996). I remember my sponsor at the time was a plumber, so he knew about as much about the music industry as I knew about plumbing. I was nervous about disclosing my problems. He said, 'You should go in and tell it like it is. Tell everyone you are two years' sober and you nearly killed yourself out there. Lay down the law of what you need'. I told them, 'I'll do the tour, but if at any time I feel squirrelly, before I pick up or use, I'll have to get out of this environment and go home. In the event of this happening, you guys are going to give me a severance package and call it a day'. Well, anybody who knows anything about the music business knows that's an unheard-of request. No one would get that deal. But remarkably I did. So I took the job with the understanding and support of the band and management and Sony."

"After completing the two-year world tour, I remember my wife telling me to take a step back and listen quietly for the answer as to what I was to do next with my life and career, to have the faith that the answer will come. I had always loved to ride a bicycle and I lost that interest, given my addiction. But when I got sober, my bicycle came back into my life. I spent about three or four months riding my bike, two hours in the morning and two hours in the evening, and I would just think about things. I thought about these two things that were a part of me: the life in recovery and this career in the music business. I waited for inspiration. After months and months of riding and just thinking about those things, Road Recovery came about. It brought the two pieces together. Road Recovery focused on the entertainment industry professionals who had dealt with their own adversity, and at-risk kids who also faced adversity. I decided to put that energy, that creativity, and that spirit, along with the experience and the exchange between these two groups, together, using live concerts and recording projects."

"It has now been over 16 years. It has been an amazing journey. We see firsthand the healing power of music. It goes beyond words to communicate between humans in a way that nothing else tangible can. How many times have we heard that somebody creates a song that goes out to the universe, and someone in a really dark place hears that song and identifies with it? That song is the very thing that keeps the person from going down their dark road. In some way or another, a connection is made, and that person no longer feels alone or isolated."

"What we do is help a collective of young people who feel like, or who have been told, they are garbage. They are disposable. Whatever they are suffering from can be expressed when a group of adults tells them, 'Hey, you're not garbage. I've been down that road. I've walked the same path that you are traveling. I've been there. But look, I got out of it. Look, these are the things that helped me move on from being that 15-year-old who wants to give up. So let's create something musical out of that'. It's powerful. All of a sudden, there is a change that occurs because something that was considered negative, horrible, and evil can be the very vehicle that has value, and a life can be turned around. All of a sudden this darkness, this whole reason for not existing, becomes light and powerful. It becomes something greater."

"When a group of people comes together and says, 'We can all draw strength from each other and we can overcome this', that is an unbelievable, magical, mystical experience. I have seen that happen a thousand times between our staff and kids, and it is an amazing process. A lot of people are afraid to go down that road and are afraid of being judged but, for those people, especially kids, who are willing to take that chance, take that leap, or that step, it can be monumental. You can use that place of being vulnerable and expressing yourself and you can fall back on that and say, 'I did that there so I can do it here', and just keep on going. We see the miracles and how lives are changed. Lives are affected on both sides . . . those who are giving and those who are taking. It is an even exchange."

"Music matters to me because . . . it requires putting out something that is inside and being vulnerable, and saying, this is mine. Music can help transcend pain and misery. It just takes you to another place."

Chapter Ten: Jeff Burger

Photo Credit: Andre Burger

Jeff Burger can't think of a time when music didn't matter to him. He also enjoys journalism, and so it's not surprising that he wound up combining his two interests. Jeff edited *Leonard Cohen on Leonard Cohen: Interviews and Encounters*, and *Springsteen on Springsteen: Interviews, Speeches, and Encounters*. He began his journalism career as a high school student and has not slowed down in more than four decades. His writing on music and many other subjects has appeared in upwards of 75 magazines, newspapers, books, and on a variety of websites, including his own, byjeffburger.com.

"I was drawn to music from a young age. When I was probably 10 years old, listening to the radio, I used to write down the Top 40 songs every week and keep track of them. Music was like a friend to me growing up. It made sense to me at times when little else did. I have always related to the Bruce Springsteen line where he sings, 'We learned more from a three-minute record than we ever learned in school'."

"I did not plan to be a journalist, but became inspired by an informal writing workshop in high school that you could go to when you had a free period. At the time I was very much into writing poetry. A teacher encouraged me, and helped me get a couple of my poems published. I got the sense of what it felt like to be published. There was also a columnist whose work I admired, and my mother, without telling me, sent some of my work to him. He said that he liked it and asked me to come in and meet with him. I did, and we kept in touch for a number of years after that. He encouraged me as I went along."

"I started writing about music in college, mainly because I loved to listen to it and couldn't afford to buy all the records I wanted. Writing was a way to get free music, because I would get review copies. In college, I majored in English, simply because I had no idea what I wanted to do. I figured an English major could read and write about all subjects, so it was a way to go forward without picking a focus. When I got out of college, I realized the only thing I knew how to do was to write, so I started moving more in that direction."

"I love just about everything about writing and editing. I have been the editor of several magazines, including *Phoenix*, the city magazine in Arizona, and now have a full-time job editing *Business Jet Traveler*, a magazine for people who travel on business jets. I have been there for 11 years. The variety is terrific. When you are the editor of a magazine, you are involved in writing, editing, working with freelancers, working with the art department and with photographers, learning about all sorts of subjects, and dealing with the Web. It's a different thing every five minutes. I love that aspect. I like the people that I work with, too."

"Journalism is a tough field at the moment. There are more people who want to do it than there are places that pay well, but it has been a wonderful field for me. I've learned a lot and enjoyed almost every minute. I would advise someone who wants to get into journalism to find somebody in the field to learn from, someone who can advise you along the way. Study the writing that you admire and see what makes it good. I would also advise forgetting graduate school. You need a college diploma, but I don't think a graduate degree is all that necessary in journalism."

"The columnist I mentioned gave me that advice. I was considering going to Medill, Northwestern University's grad school for journalism. At the time it cost $6,000 a year. I wrote to my columnist friend and said, 'What do you think I should do?' He wrote back: 'Save the $6,000 and get out in the real world'. That turned out to be good advice."

"I think the best interviews are the ones that go beyond the formal Q&A, where it's more like a conversation between two friends. Interviewing Wolfman Jack was a highlight for me. I talked with him in the 1970s. It was late at night after an Eagles concert. He told me all these colorful stories of his early days in radio. Another memorable conversation was with drummer Spencer Dryden. He played in major 1950s rock bands and then in the Jefferson Airplane and later in New Riders of the Purple Sage, so he had quite a few tales to tell. I recently interviewed Daymond John, who is from the TV show 'Shark Tank'. That was fascinating, too. He started with nothing and became a multimillionaire with his clothing line."

"Of course, my Springsteen interview was fascinating. That's in my book on him. I got to interview him before he became famous. In the conversation, he talked about how he and his band were struggling and making only $75 each a week. He said he worried that money pressures would force some of his group members to quit, but he told me that he'd keep making music no matter what. That's kind of how I felt about being a journalist."

"Music matters to me because . . . it speaks to me on a deeper level than any other art form. A song can be exhilarating and moving and it can transport us to many places, including wherever we were when we first heard it. At its best, music is emotion turned into sound."

Chapter Eleven: Henry Butler

Henry Butler grew up in the Calliope Projects in New Orleans. Blinded by glaucoma at birth, he never let his background nor his disability hinder his curiosity. He took to piano at six, and by 14 was performing professionally. He has been called "the greatest proponent of the classic New Orleans Piano Tradition", but his ability to push the boundaries is what makes him so remarkable. Henry received his Master's in music from Michigan State. He learned from the Jazz greats and continues in their legacy. He is also a top photographer who has exhibited nationally and internationally. Henry was selected for HBO's documentary on the Art of Blind Photographers, and is an educator and advocate for the blind. He seeks life outside his comfort level, and recently formed the Hot 9 band and revitalized Impulse Recording.

"Music for me was a way out of the ghetto. It was also a tool for visiting other communities and getting away from the segregated environment that I was born in. It was a tool for discovering other cultures, and for learning about other cultures. It was a tool for learning. It helped me learn to focus. It helped me with math. It helped me with all kinds of things. It was an inspiring tool."

"Through my music, I have met many people who have inspired me. Through my music, I've been able to visit wonderful places where I've been inspired to do things that I, at least before any of those visits, never thought I would be able to do. I've had great teachers who have inspired me. George Duke showed me how to use both hands to go in contrary directions. He was just a great teacher. Harold Mabern is a jazz pianist and was also an inspiring teacher of mine. Alvin Batiste was probably the best coach I had in college, the best teacher, because he didn't only work with me musically in the Jazz area, but he was like a father away from home. He inspired me to study all kinds of things. These teachers inspired me to do what I do. They wanted me to carry the banner forward, and continue to share my talents with others, especially younger musicians. They inspired me to be a source of inspiration to other people."

"Through my training I've come to realize that, depending on how you play certain chords and harmonies, you can touch each person differently. There are specific things you can do in music to help you realize happiness, and sadness. There are certain things in music that you can do and it will make you say to yourself, 'I don't know if I want to play it again or hear that again or feel those emotions again'. It helps if you're really at a level where you can do this, or you can realize this. It's a great tool of realization, a great tool for self-study."

"Also, as you're studying music in school, you realize what a great tool it is for helping with concentration, keeping your mind focused. It can wind up being a great study tool for anything else. Most of the people I know who studied music, even if they lived in ghetto areas or they lived in some of the more expensive types of communities, never got in trouble if they actually studied music throughout most of their schooling. For people who lived in ghettos, it was usually a way for them to work themselves out of those places."

"The mindset I put myself in before each concert or performance is one of inspiration. I want to uplift, encourage, and in some way inform – maybe even heal, if that's possible – anybody who's listening to what we do. I believe music can do all of those things. I know, for me, music has provided me with opportunities. Music has informed me. It has inspired me, and of course, uplifted me; it's done great things for me. I figure if music has done so much for me, it can do something for a lot of people. I always hope I can be a positive source for those who are listening."

"It was pretty tough after Katrina to keep a semblance of normalcy. Katrina devastated our facilities for my camp for blind teenage musicians. I lost everything I had. I lost my house, my 1925 vintage piano, most of my scores and recordings; most of my stuff. There was over eight feet of water. But music helped me realize how important living was. I had to persevere. I did go through a period of PTSD. It was tough not to feel sadness almost all the time. I think one of the great lessons I learned was that human beings have to be able to detach themselves from possessions. It was the lesson I learned from suffering through Katrina's devastation."

"I see the value of music and apply the principles of focus, practice, discipline, perseverance, and release in everything I do. At some point in our life, we should learn – and must learn – varying degrees of detachment, because we are going to lose things. Maybe everybody won't lose as much as I lost, but you're going to lose boyfriends, or girlfriends. You're going to lose keys and going to lose books. You're going to lose all kinds of things and as a result you will need to quickly detach yourself, especially if you realize after a time that you can't find whatever it is you've lost. I realized that I had to go on, and if I was going to be an inspiration to anybody, I had to overcome those losses and start over; which I did and which I am continuing to do. You know, life doesn't end because you lose things. It's only physical, material things. Just as one loses a material thing, one can gain new material things if that's what a person wants. I learned great lessons through the storm, and my life has been wonderful ever since."

"Music matters to me because . . . it brings joy, it brings hope, it brings love, it brings information. Music gives me a tool where I can go to all kinds of places and share a wonderful spirit of joy, of love, of hope, of transformation. I can share this with people in jails or universities, in high

49

schools or the White House, in Carnegie Concert Hall or Avery Fisher at Lincoln Center. It doesn't matter where I am. I can go anywhere and I can inspire by giving the gift of music to all the people who are willing to listen."

Chapter Twelve: Michael Cartellone

Michael Cartellone is a study in contrasts. Musically gifted, he is a multi-platinum recording artist and the drummer for Lynyrd Skynyrd, a hard rocking all-American band he joined in 1998. He has worked with a varied range of musical artists, from Cher to Peter Frampton. Artistically gifted, he is a well-respected visual artist who creates thought-provoking, dynamic canvases. He has also painted artwork for a children's clothing line and classical album covers. This creative diversity brings an excited energy to his work, whether it is through a drumstick or a paintbrush.

"Music and art both played major roles in my life as a kid growing up in Cleveland, Ohio. Aside from dabbling as a magician and playing some baseball, I spent all my time drumming, painting, or drawing."

"It was my kindergarten teacher who noticed I had some painting and drawing ability when I was just four, and suggested to my parents that they encourage it. So, my parents enrolled me that summer in the Cleveland Institute of Art, and I've never stopped working on my craft. My musical interest began when I was nine years old, inspired by my older cousin, Bert, who was a great drummer. I used to beg him to let me play his drums every time we would visit his house. I think my parents realized how serious I was about drumming and decided to arrange lessons with Bert's teacher. That was it for me . . . no turning back. By the time I was 11, my drum teacher, who also played accordion and had a polka band, invited me to play with him at a bar one night. It was my first professional gig and I made three dollars that night . . . by the way, I've worked for less, since!"

"So, like painting, I began drumming as a young kid and I've never stopped working on either. It has been a wonderful lifelong journey."

"I'm lucky that my schedule allows me to do both, simultaneously. When I'm on tour I always bring a canvas and paints into the hotel rooms where I stay. The quiet, introspective painting during the day and the loud, public drumming at night, naturally create their own balance. For me, art and music are both very personal expressions and represent two halves of a whole. They enhance, support, and motivate each other. I can't imagine doing only one. Drumming and painting satisfy my creative needs on different levels, and in different ways. Again, the two are a perfect balance."

"As for inspiration, I find it everywhere. Artistically, I'm inspired by life experiences. My eyes are always open for something that could trigger a new idea. Musically, I'm inspired from hearing and seeing all kinds of music performed. I should mention that my art is not spontaneous in any way. I take time planning and researching for each new painting. This approach gives me peace of mind, so when I begin a painting there is no guesswork. For my most recent paintings, 'The Four Davids', which are based on the famous Michelangelo statue, it took me several years of planning, research, and sketching. I wanted to present 100 years of art history and that took time. Also, I'm usually thinking ahead. I always have a painting in progress, but quite often I'm planning the next one before I finish what I'm working on. Currently, I am halfway through a painting, but already have the next six planned."

"Music matters to me because . . . it enables me to express myself using a universal language. And in a way, I can say that same thing about my art."

Chapter Thirteen: Mark Churchill

Mark Churchill wears many hats. He is an educator, conductor, cellist, and Dean Emeritus and Senior Advisor of the renowned New England Conservatory. He started numerous music organizations, including the Youth Orchestra of the Americas, which draws gifted students from North and South America. Perhaps his most important position has been Director of El Sistema, USA. This program expands music education globally, and Mark is the perfect person to accomplish this goal.

"It was a 6th grade music teacher who introduced me to music. She was a very avid musician, and played piano and recordings as part of our curriculum. I chose the cello and off I went. I didn't come from a musical family, so I didn't think I would be in music. I started late and didn't have the most privileged musical education. I had a wonderful high school program and college program at a small public college. I had the normal stuff that existed at the time, but not one that is commonly associated with formal musical training. I could very much relate to El Sistema program because of my background and became actively involved in the global movement in the late 1990s."

"The El Sistema movement was launched in Venezuela 40 years ago, by Dr. José Abreu. As an economist, politician, and musician, he felt that young musicians of his country, who wanted to become professional, classical musicians, didn't have a system to play together and experience the social aspect of music-making. The music programs at that time in Venezuela focused exclusively on solo playing and musical academics. Remarkably, Dr. Abreu held the first rehearsal of the first youth orchestra that would grow into El Sistema in a parking garage, and only 11 students showed up! But the orchestra grew very rapidly and in two years became a world-class youth orchestra that won a major competition in Scotland. Dr.

Abreu saw that the power of playing in orchestras collectively and making music together would be a very effective way of addressing one of the major challenges in his country: poverty and lack of education for underserved and underprivileged children."

"From the first experience of that initial youth orchestra, he established a fantastic vision where learning music in groups in an intensive way could lift people out of their economically-challenged personal conditions. He set up free programs for young people all over the country. They were intense music education centers that met every day of the week."

"By establishing youth orchestras in very poor communities that didn't have music as a part of their culture, these kids were exposed to caring, supportive, and protective adults. Once these young students were in the program, they learned how to relate to music at a very personal level. Music instilled a sense of hope and possibility for them, creating what Dr. Abreu refers to as an 'affluence of the spirit'."

"Today this system serves some 500,000 students in Venezuela alone. There are also hundreds of centers all over the world, with everything from orchestras, choruses, folk and jazz ensembles, as well as special needs programs. They are serving a large percentage of the most challenged kids and families in Venezuela, and are really transforming their lives. The powerful idea to use excellence-driven music education and performance as a tool for social transformation has captured the imagination of educators, musicians and social leaders throughout the world."

"In 2006, El Sistema was described by Simon Rattle, conductor of the

Berlin Philharmonic, as the most important thing happening in music in the world today, and this statement energized the process of the globalization of El Sistema. When I got involved 15 years ago, I said, 'We have to do everything we can to try to shine a spotlight on this and position it to inspire others to do likewise'. This led to the development of a close relationship between the New England Conservatory and El Sistema, which included a signed friendship agreement, student collaborations and faculty exchanges. Soon El Sistema USA and the Abreu Fellows leadership-training program were launched. We now have over 100 El Sistema-inspired programs in the U.S., with a number of new ones about to be launched next year. Given the scope of our country, it isn't huge, but the results in a short time are showing themselves to be very significant. As part of a worldwide movement, it is something to pay attention to."

"What is so exciting about El Sistema in the United States is that no one owns it and nobody needs to give permission to open a center. It is a leaderless movement which is open to all. Most programs are sponsored by orchestras, but others are part of a variety of other non-profits or independently incorporated organizations. We have eight programs in the Boston area alone. The largest one at the Conservatory Lab Charter School has 450 elementary-age children who perform and study music five days a week and play in one of six orchestras. The top group recently did a side-by-side performance with a professional orchestra. They played in the same venue where the Boston Pops plays on the Fourth of July. It's so magical to see the confidence these students gain and to see their potential capacity to build an exciting future for themselves through music."

"Recently I spoke with a group of 4th and 5th graders who want to be doctors, politicians, or other professionals. They see no limit to their future yet they come from backgrounds of extremely limited resources. You see this in all the El Sistema music programs, and it's very energizing. Most of us are highly trained musicians, and it gives us real hope that this treasure that we've devoted ourselves to and deeply believe in can have a transformational effect on all children, regardless of their backgrounds."

"Music matters to me because . . . it is the language of the human soul. It has a very central place in human expression. There is evidence that we sang before we spoke and communicated verbally in our evolutionary development. It's easy to see that for young babies, music is central to their experience in the world. And learning music engages the physical, emotional, intellectual, social and spiritual, everything it means to be human, in an exquisite balance which supports all we do in our lives."

Chapter Fourteen: Charles Connor

Charles Connor was born in New Orleans in 1935. He knew he wanted to be a drummer before he could express it in words. Music and hard work went hand in hand. Practicing for hours on end would bring opportunity during a time in history where options were limited. He would play with some of the legends like Sam Cooke, The Coasters, Jackie Wilson, and James Brown. But Charles is best known for being Little Richard's drummer, a gig that started when he was just 18.

"My father always told me that when my mother was carrying me in her womb, every time she was around music I would jump to the beat in her stomach. My mother thought that I would be a dancer or a musician or something involving music, because I would get so excited when I would hear it. I took to music early. I grew up one block west of Bourbon Street up in New Orleans. When I was young I used to tap dance for the white tourists. They'd drop some coins and watch me perform. We didn't have much money, but when I was five years old my father bought me a little set of drums because he thought that I had rhythm. The set contained a bass drum, a snare drum, and a cymbal. I used to play those drums all the time. I dreamed of becoming a professional drummer."

"When I was 15 years old, I played my first gig. It was with Professor Longhair for the 1950 Mardi Gras. He was a popular New Orleans blues singer and pianist. One of his band members, a much older guy, couldn't make the gig because he got drunk, so they asked me to drum in with the band. They were famous for the song, 'Go to the Mardi Gras'. I played around New Orleans and in a bunch of little country towns with them for almost a year. I was paying my dues in Nashville, Tennessee playing with a small group called Shirley and Lee. They had a big song out called 'Come On Baby, Let the Good Times Roll'. They would sing and I played my drums with them."

"I played with a lot of musicians along the way before I met Little Richard. One night we were playing in a club and Little Richard was in a club about a half a block from us. He had about 200 people at the club, called The New Era Club. We didn't draw much of a crowd at the club I was playing in. We had about 13 people in the club and that included the band, bartender, and waitress. Just by chance Little Richard came out to that club and heard me play. I guess he liked what he heard because he asked to see me. He said, 'Tell the drummer that I want to see him. Have him come to the YMCA tomorrow and by the way, bring the other guy, too'. The other guy was named Wilbur Smith. His professional name was Lee Diamond."

"Wilbur Smith and I and went to the YMCA the very next day. Little Richard met us and asked straight out if we'd join his band. Well, I was 18 and couldn't believe what I was hearing. The drum set I was playing belonged to the club and I had hotel bills to pay and holes in my shoes. I wasn't making much money. When Little Richard said, 'I would like to bring you guys back to Macon, Georgia'. Little Richard was originally from there. I said, 'Yeah, that sounds good and everything, but please could you feed us because we haven't had a decent meal in about three weeks'. He said sure and stood up right then and sent out for some stew meat, black-eyed peas, collard greens, and all that sort of stuff."

"Little Richard had been really good to me already and so after we ate that most delicious meal I said, 'Now I don't mind going back to Macon but I have three problems'. He said, 'What are your problems?' I had to tell him that the drums I was playing on were not my drums. I also told him I was three weeks behind on my hotel rent and that I had holes in my shoes. He said, 'No problem. I'll take care of that bill. I will pay your three weeks rent and I will get you some drums at the pawnshop. And when we get to Macon, I will buy you some shoes'. I couldn't believe it but he did all of that. He really helped me when I was at my lowest point. I could have gone back home and everything, but I would have been mad at myself. Instead, Little Richard called my mother and asked her if I could travel with him. And she said, 'Well, of course, it's Little Richard!' That was in 1953. I was 18 years old and Little Richard was 20."

"We got to Macon, Georgia and the next day Little Richard let us rest up. The day after he said, 'I want to bring you to the Macon, Georgia train station'. I said, 'For what?' He said, 'Just come to the train station'. So I went and he had me listen to the trains because he wanted to put that sound in his music. He knew the sound, but he did not know the value. He did not know how to explain what kind of notes those were. When the train pulls off, it goes 'choo, choo, choo, choo, choo'. Those are eighth notes. That day in 1953 was when I created the 'choo choo train beat'. Millions of drummers are playing that beat today and they don't know that it originated from me in the Macon, Georgia train station."

"Little Richard was a sharp-minded businessman. He introduced rock 'n' roll to the white honky-tonk clubs and that wasn't easy to do. In the 1950s, white and black musicians could not even play together. You could play in their club, but you could not go through the front door. You had to go through the back door. Even though the white club owners thought Little Richard had a great show, we had to follow special rules in the white club. We could not look macho or nothing like that. We had to look feminine so folks wouldn't think we were going to mingle with the white girls. Little Richard had us dress in loud clothes. We had to wear the pancake makeup and all that feminine stuff. Some of us got our hair curled in the beauty shop like a woman. Me and about two or three other guys in the band did that. We couldn't risk looking too macho. We were straight and everything, but that's the way we had to look to play in the white clubs."

"I also played with James Brown. But that's the thing, Little Richard was creating a certain style of rock music that was different from everyone else. In 1956, 'Keep a Knockin'' was a big hit. Little Richard was the first to use a four-bar drum intro for a rock 'n' roll record. That record sold thousands and thousands of copies, and Little Richard gave me a thousand dollars of that money for creating a four-bar drum intro on that rock 'n' roll record."

"'Tutti Frutti' is another one of his famous songs. He used to sing 'Tutti Frutti' in the club when there were no children, only adults. He had two versions. For the record we made it was 'Tutti Fruitti, all rooty' not 'great booty'. Then you heard him yell, 'A-wop-bop-a-loo-mop-a-lomp-bam-boom!' Well, that was him explaining my drum parts in words. That's how that line came about."

"We toured all over the U.S. and in Canada. I was 20 and it was 1955. We played the major theaters like the Howard Theater in Washington, D.C., the Apollo Theater in Harlem, and the Paramount Theater in Brooklyn. We played around the world, too. We played in Japan and in the Philippines. We played the whole country of Australia. We played in Sweden, Denmark, and in most of Europe. They liked American music in Europe. This was around the time of Buddy Holly and Elvis Presley. Those musicians didn't have to deal with the racial prejudice like we did. Elvis was accepted because he was a white man, even though he danced like a black man with all that shaking. It was a life-changing experience to be a part of history at that time in the world, and to see the youth rebellion that was taking place through rock 'n' roll music."

"Music matters to be because . . . it makes you feel good. You can play music in any country and even if you don't know the words, the melody makes you feel something. You can communicate with music."

Chapter Fifteen: Bill Conti

Photo Credit: David Hartig

Bill Conti grew up in a musical family, but having musical genes doesn't necessarily translate to the accomplished success he has achieved. Bill began learning piano at age seven from his father and found the passion that would take him to Louisiana State University, where he received a Bachelor of music in piano and composition. He went on to The Julliard School of Music where he received another music degree as well as a Master's degree. He is recognized as one of the most esteemed composers and conductors for Hollywood. In 1989 he received a star on the Hollywood Walk of Fame. He has won five Emmys, three of them for Outstanding Musical Direction for directing the Academy Awards, which he did for 19 years until 2003, the most of any musical director. He has also won an Academy Award for Best Original Score for "The Right Stuff". The movie list of scores he has created reads like a who's who. Some of these include: "The Karate Kid", "Broadcast News", "Private Benjamin", and of course "Rocky", the movie that won the 1976 Academy Award for Best Picture. He composed the music for all but one of the film's sequels. His TV work is also impressive and showcases some of the most memorable theme songs of the decades. There were hits such as "Dynasty", "Falcon Crest", "Lifestyles of the Rich and Famous", and "Cagney and Lacey". He also wrote the songs for ABC's "Good Morning America", "World News Tonight", "Prime Time Live", "Nightline", "ABC Sports", and "Inside Edition". In 2013 he joined the San Diego Symphony as its principal pops conductor.

"Music played a tremendous role in my life growing up, because my grandfather and my father were musicians. Eating, breathing, walking, talking, and music were all in the same category. No one thought about music as something different. Everyone did it, or practiced it, or studied it. Music was just a part of our life. In my house when I was a kid, the focus was not whether you practiced or not, but how long you practiced. This

66

was much different than hearing, 'Stop practicing; you're giving me a headache!' I was very lucky to have music in my life at an early age."

"When I was in high school, I began playing in a nightclub. In those days nightclubs had bands. I was 14 years old and I thought that playing in the nightclub was a big deal. By the time I was 16 or 17, it was time to decide whether to go to college or not. I was not so sure that I shouldn't continue on my nightclub path and go to another saloon and play music. My father was my mentor and I knew he would support me in my decision to begin my own life and continue in my own way when I was 17 and graduating from high school. He cared enough to say maybe I should reconsider. In other words, he thought that I could be a better musician. He thought that maybe at 17 I was settling for less by not furthering my musical education. That was my 'ah ha moment' when I decided to continue studying, and I earned a Master's and a doctorate in music."

"I feel that as a musician you are supposed to do something with your music. A musician who plays or practices does not do it in a vacuum. He does the practicing pretty much in a vacuum, but performing, playing music, and having music touch people, reach people, communicate with people--that's where those important connections happen. Music is not about the thinking process. Sometimes music just comes in and grips you and you feel excited. You feel happy. Sometimes you feel like you're going to cry. As a musician, when you can reach people emotionally, then you will have moments when you are doing what you are supposed to be doing. And over the years, I have always done something with my music. I think if people have heard your music and have been moved by your music, then you are fulfilling one of the jobs of the musician."

"I've been able to use my music for a variety of media, and each is different in terms of the production aspect and the audience. When writing soundtracks for a movie, there is a lot of give and take. The composer on a film will sit with the director and decide where the music will go. They will agree on the emotional content of what is supposed to be happening in the scene. It might be transition music just to pass the time. It might be music to make characters fall in love. Of course you also have to think about the movie audience. People come to movies by choice and they want to be there. They've bought a ticket and are sitting down waiting for our story. The movie audience has been captured, and so we have that attention. It is different for a TV audience or a live audience."

"When I created the soundtrack for the first 'Rocky' movie, it was inspirational music. For the most famous song, though, the music for the preparation scene before the big fight came together piecemeal. In the tenth reel, the director, John Avildsen, asked me to write about a minute and a half's worth of music so that he could cut the film and put together the montage of Rocky working out before the big fight. I gave it to him, but as it turned out, he had shot reels of Rocky training and wanted to use more footage. He said, 'Can you give me another 30 seconds?' And so I pieced together another 30 seconds, and then he wanted another 30. We ended up working our way from about a minute and a half to double that. By the end we had about three minutes of something that sounded like a song. He asked me, 'Can't we say something about what Rocky is doing now?' I said, 'You can do anything you want. It's your movie'. Since we had two lyricists on the project we got to work and they wrote the lyrics to it. No one sat down and wrote the song in the sense that it was going to be a song from the beginning. It was supposed to be a minute and a half of training and it evolved into the training song, 'Gonna Fly Now'."

"Now with a TV show, it is an entirely different process. The audience is not captured. You can turn the TV on or off. The producer of that TV show wants to grab the attention of the potential viewer. The producer will tell the composer to work off the show's main title and incorporate a tease. In other words, figure out the reason why you are going to watch this show when you have never seen it before."

"TV shows have a much different agenda than movies. It is not a slow, once upon a time type of storytelling. It is quick and immediate. It's like selling cars and candy bars. In my case, for the shows like *Dynasty*, *Cagney and Lacey* and *Falcon Crest*, that I created the music for, they all began with an idea. The producer would tell me, in the case of *Dynasty*, it is going to focus on rich people in Denver, Colorado. It is going to be elegant. My job was to describe those emotions and the feeling of the main title through music. For *Cagney and Lacey*, the producer said I shouldn't emphasize that it was a cop show because the show followed a comedy in the TV lineup. A cop show has a much different feel. It is darker and edgier. He wanted to keep people who were listening to the comedy tuned in to stay and watch this show, and so I focused more on lightness for the theme. *Dynasty*, *Falcon Crest*, *Lifestyles of the Rich and Famous*, and all of these and the other shows that I did the theme songs for had certain agendas that I needed to follow with my music. I needed to tell the audience from the title that flashed across the screen who was in the show, what it was about, and what it felt like."

"Now for the work I do as conductor with the San Diego Symphony, it is also immediate, like TV, but in a different fashion. For movies and even for TV, if the director does not like an aspect of it, he can ask for a change. We can talk about it and rework it and record it again, but when you are performing music for people who are sitting in the audience, that can't happen. What you are creating with the musicians is something live. For me, when everything comes together in a live performance, it feels as if the essence of the composer who wrote the music, his soul, his emotions, everything about him is with me."

"Whether I'm conducting a piece by Mozart or not, the feelings are the same. It is a comingling of sound and emotion among the musicians, the composer, the conductor, and the audience who hear the finished result. All that energy and intent is being put out to ears that have come to listen and are responsive, because no one forced them to attend a concert. It is a wonderful feeling to be able to express this musical oneness and communicate these feelings of coming together on an emotional level if not something higher than that. It is a lot of fun to be working with the best musicians in their profession and doing your best. The maximum effort is being put out. When you walk away you feel pretty good, because you have done your best and you hope that everyone who participated by playing and listening has enjoyed the experience."

"Music matters to me because . . . it's my life force."

Chapter Sixteen: Brian Dallow

Music Soothes the Soul   Matthew Bernstein

Music has always been a part of Brian Dallow's world. A child
prodigy in piano, he excelled in the art. His exposure to the world of music
at a young age made an impression on him. As an adult, he started Music
for All Seasons with his wife, Rena Fruchter, to help people confined to
facilities and institutions, including homeless shelters, hospitals, and jails.
He brings music into people's lives. Music for All Seasons has received
numerous commendations and awards, including several NEA grants.
They perform over 250 live concerts per year in New Jersey, Connecticut,
California, and Pennsylvania.

"Both my wife and I are professional musicians. We have been
musicians all of our lives. We are both pianists. We started playing as
children. We shared a similar experience as we were child prodigies but
from two different countries. My wife was born in the United States and I
was born in England. We spent our entire lives in the music world and in
the music industry, experiencing its numerous benefits."

"About 25 years ago, we realized there were many people who are
essentially shut out from the world of music, and those people were
confined in institutions. These people may be in hospitals. They may be
prisoners. They may be in halfway houses. They may be in shelters. This
music-less condition can exist anywhere. We wanted to provide that
access for these people. It started out with simply providing programs of a
very high quality for residential facilities. Word spread and the program
grew to provide benefits to very specific types of populations."

"One of the primary populations we work with is children of domestic
violence. When children are exposed to the trauma that is a product of
domestic violence, they tend to shut down from their parents and from
their peers. They even shut down from their siblings in the family setting.

Children of domestic violence become very introverted. They do not talk or interact in the same way that normal children will interact with either adults or peers. In our program, we utilize music to break down some of those barriers. Our goal is to create an environment where they can feel comfortable enough to make music. We break music down to a very simple form. Sometimes it's as simple as using a shaker, or a piece of production equipment."

"We discovered that when children of domestic violence start working together in groups, whether with siblings, other kids, their parents, or staff members, they form a connection. Music breaks down inhibitions, providing opportunities for these children to interact. They begin to talk a little bit more. Some of the initial barriers are broken down, positively affecting their ability to function in classrooms. It certainly is not a magic bullet, but it does assist in the process of reversing trauma over time."

"The other area that we work with is a new program that we created three years ago called Voices of Valor®. It specifically addresses the issue of trauma for veterans, mostly from Iraq and Afghanistan. In many cases, veterans are suffering from posttraumatic stress and also from severe traumatic brain injury. One of the first things we learned through research was that writing down a traumatic experience can be therapeutic. It is a means of getting it out and putting it into a different container, as opposed to holding it inside the body. The second thing we learned is that writing made it easier for the veterans to discuss those experiences with people who have undergone similar traumatic events. Through discussion in a staffed group setting, we make it possible to turn those emotions and feelings into a song."

"We incorporated this powerful concept into a musical program in which we take eight to ten veterans over a period of about eight weeks. We meet once a week with two musician facilitators and a psychologist. These educators and health care professionals work with the group through a variety of processes. We have a specific week-by-week curriculum. At the end of about seven weeks, the veterans go into a recording studio to create a song. The veterans work with musicians, producers, singers, and writers to produce a song. About a week later, we have a celebration with friends and families. Each veteran sings the song he or she created."

"Singing is an extremely cathartic process, on a number of levels. First of all, the veterans have created a sense of community, and bonded with a group of strangers who have shared a similar experience to theirs. The group provides them with a support system. Second, the veterans experience the transformative power of music. They exchange experiences which are, for the most part, negative, and then each turns his or her negative experiences into something positive and creative. One of the issues veterans face is that they feel the need to hide these traumatic experiences from family and friends. This program breaks down some of those barriers. It gives veterans an opportunity to start talking about some of those difficult experiences in a new format. The process is extremely rewarding. We hope that the positive feelings that come out of the Voices of Valor® program will be incorporated into other parts of these veterans' lives."

"Music matters to be because . . . it is the fundamental voice in my life. It is the means by which I express myself."

Chapter Seventeen: Deekron

Deekron Krikorian, known as The Fitness DJ, had a passion for music from a young age. As a life-long athlete and music lover, he understood the benefits of working out to music. Fast forward to business school at University of Michigan in 1999. Next it was consulting at top New York firms. Once Deekron had assembled all the skills he needed to start his own company, he knew he wanted to create something that made a difference in people's lives. He founded Motion Traxx in 2009, which combines fitness and music to improve workouts and ultimately people's health.

"My life revolved around music. I grew up in the 1980s and loved playing the drums. Music was my form of self-expression. I liked heavy metal. That genre became a really great topic for me to meet and talk to people about this new band or that new album. When I was in school, a couple of my buddies started a music business where they would record concerts and we would talk for hours about that slick solo or what have you. Besides bonding with my friends, music also helped me connect with my brother. We had very different personalities and we were five years apart in age but he was always into music. The one thing that brought us together was talking and listening to music."

"Motion Traxx really developed from my love for music. My dad was a professional athlete so I grew up playing sports. To stay fit I'd go to the gym and I always used my brother's music for my workouts. As we all know, going to the gym and running on a treadmill for a half hour or having to lift weights for an hour can get dull, so I would use music to inspire and motivate me. It really worked! I got the inspiration to use the positive energy from music to motivate people to work out and be more fit."

"We team up with top fitness trainers to create audio workouts that feature voiceover coaching and motivating dance music. The audio workouts are specially designed for cardio machines, like the treadmill, and help people get more from their workouts. For example, if a routine has a warm up and cool down period then we will have music that is appropriate for that and does not push people hard right away. When the time comes to push hard, the music builds in tempo and intensity and really drives you. If there is a recovery phase within a workout, the music also follows along. It becomes your guide. People have a much better workout using Motion Traxx than just working out with their own music or just streaming music, because it provides a guided workout routine set to music that's synced with the workout."

"I've realized that with launching any business you have to work hard and usually on your own. You are wearing a lot of hats. You have to do all the things the business requires with very little money at first. So it is important to feel passionate about what you are doing because it is hard work. I love what I do. What I like best is working with the trainers and being able to translate their thoughts for motivation into music. That part is really exciting for me. I like thinking through a workout and wondering, 'How do I get the right track for this section of the workout?' or 'How do I push people hard right now because the trainer wants them to push at their max in this section?' It's about bringing in the right track at the right time. So programming music and making it match what the trainer wants is really interesting for me. It's a very creative process and one that makes me think."

"The testimonials I receive are very inspiring to me. A woman emailed me saying that before she found Motion Traxx she could not even run a mile, but now she runs all the time and just signed up for her first half marathon. Those powerful testimonials like hers come from people all over the world. I get emails from the Philippines. I get emails from South Africa. It has been pretty awesome to see the impact Motion Traxx has had on people's lives."

"It is also exciting for us as a small company to get the attention of bigger brands. We did a really big project for Gatorade a few years back, which was really awesome. It came at a time when we were starting to run out of money and things were not looking too good. We weren't sure if we were going to make it, but Gatorade was launching a new product and they partnered with us. We worked with their ambassador-trainers and recorded audio workouts that they gave away to help promote their new Gatorade products. It was a great success story that I am proud of, because we turned the corner after that."

"Music matters to me because . . . it's my life."

Chapter Eighteen: Geert D'hollander

Geert D'hollander is "one of the finest carillonneurs in the world." From a young age he studied piano. This led to chamber music, choral and orchestral direction, fugue and composition at the Royal Conservatory in Antwerp, Belgium, and carillon at the Royal Carillon School in Mechelen, Belgium. His resume is studded with awards. In 2008, he was awarded the Berkeley Medal of Honor for Distinguished Service to the Carillon. He has also placed first in more than 30 international competitions for carillon or composition. He has taught at some of the finest institutions, and frequently gives Master Classes throughout Europe and the U.S. He is a sought-after performer who performs all over the world. In October 2012, Geert was named Bok Tower Gardens' only fourth full-time carillonneur.

"Music was always playing in my house when I was growing up. My father was a pianist, organist, and carillonneur. He taught music and so the piano was played daily. I think that was why I always knew I was going to be doing something with music when I grew up. For a while I thought it was going to be playing the piano. I also thought about composition. But really from the age of seventeen, I knew it was going to be the carillon."

"Being a carillonneur is rare. The study takes about four to six years. One can study at different universities in the U.S. or in private schools in Europe. There are only a couple of hundred people worldwide who play the instrument. But there are fewer than 100 worldwide professional carillonneurs and there are only a handful of full-time positions."

"The Guild of Carillonneurs in North America officially defines the instrument as follows: 'A carillon consists of a series of at least 23 tuned bells, played from a keyboard that allows expressiveness through variation in touch, and on which the player, or carillonneur, can play a broad range of music—from arrangements of popular and classical music to original compositions created just for the carillon. Carillon bells can be heard throughout North America, in cities, at churches, on school campuses, in public parks, and in many other places where people gather'."

"The carillon I play at Bok Tower Gardens has 60 bells (five octaves), ranging in weight from 16 lbs to 11+ tons. The total weight is 63+ tons. Carillon bells are stationary; only the clapper on the inside of the bell moves. In 1928, the John Taylor Bellfoundry, Ltd. of Loughborough, England, which still makes bells today, designed and built the instrument. It is housed in a Florida coquina stone and Georgian grey marble tower. It is very ornate. Milton B. Medary, a renowned American architect, designed it."

"Bok Tower Gardens is definitely one of the most unique carillon towers in the world. In fact, when I graduated from the Royal Carillon School in Mechelen, Belgium, my father promised to show me the most magical carillon place he knew, and that turned out to be Bok Tower Gardens. So when we came here to visit, I played this instrument more than 30 years ago, not knowing that one day it would be 'my tower'."

"A typical day for me finds me in my office in the tower. I quickly check my email and then start composing and arranging pieces for a couple of hours. In the afternoon I digitize my scores, study at the practice keyboard, and perform two programmed concerts."

"When I play, it is magical. It relaxes me completely. I forget everything else while playing. The music completely absorbs me. I hope I convey that feeling. I hope listeners enjoy my music and, for a second, forget about the hectic world we live in."

"Music matters to me because . . . it is my life. It's why I'm here."

Chapter Nineteen: Jacob Edgar

Photo Credit: Mike Worthington

Jacob Edgar is a global adventurer. He travels the globe, exploring the diverse ways people express themselves through music. As the host of *Music Voyager*, a music and travel television series broadcast on PBS stations, he features innovative musical talent from around the world; the same types of musical talents his musically-progressive parents exposed him to as a child. Jacob spent hours digging through their hip, eclectic record collection of reggae, folk, and African sounds. This love of the world's music led him to pursue a Master's Degree in Ethnomusicology from UCLA. In 2006, he founded the record label Cumbancha.

"It's an indescribably amazing experience to be able to travel the world as the host for a television program focused on music. Wherever you go, the red carpet is rolled out for you, because, for some reason, everywhere around the world, people are just enchanted by TV. When you come as part of a TV show, people give you access to incredible opportunities."

"I've been in magical settings in some of the most picturesque locations in the world. For example, I've done an unplugged performance with Etana, an incredible singer from Jamaica, on Goldeneye beach in Jamaica, where Ian Fleming wrote his Bond novels. I've been in the middle of the Negev Desert in Israel, where they set up a stage for 5000 people, for a performance by the Idan Raichel Project, which fuses Hebrew texts with Arab and Ethiopian music. Imagine being surrounded by pillars of stone cliffs as the backdrop, with thousands of Israelis singing along to a song performed in Arabic. I've had more than my share of incredible life experiences for one lifetime. It's like living in an I-MAX movie."

"I believe that music is an important tool for helping people communicate with each other, for helping them learn about other cultures, and for helping to accept and appreciate the differences that we have, as well as our similarities. I never want to give people the impression that, because I think a song is great, that they can't like something else."

"In my travels, I try to look for music that has a universal quality. I want it to appeal to people like me - fanatics and freaks about music who are interested in unusual quirky things - as well as music that would also to appeal to my grandmother. Usually that comes down to a really strong melody, something that grabs you quickly, and something that isn't so esoteric that it won't just turn you off. I'm really trying to find the musical doorways. I want to make people feel like this world is accessible to them and, at the same time, I want to be authentic. I want the music I share to be music of soul, creativity, and culture."

"Music matters to me because . . . it reflects where we come from and where we are going."

Chapter Twenty: Michael Franti

Michael Franti is multi-talented. He plays the guitar, he sings, he writes but, perhaps, most importantly, he is driven to make a positive impact in the world. Whether that is accomplished through his popular band, Michael Franti & Spearhead, his social activism, the Do It For The Love Foundation he founded, or his philanthropic support of numerous causes, Michael believes in making a difference by helping others.

"Music was an escape for me. I grew up in a small college town and I would listen to the campus radio station at night. The music took my mind to places in the world that I never imagined that I would ever go. It introduced me to new sounds and different cultures and political ideas. It became my medicine."

"At fifteen, I went to a Linton Kwesi Johnson concert. He was a reggae artist from England. He walked on stage and read a poem a cappella. Then, the band kicked in behind him and he did the exact same poem to the music. I was blown away by the power of his presence and the power of his words. I decided at that moment that was what I wanted to do. I wanted to bring poetry to music."

"It wasn't until I went to the University of San Francisco that I started playing music. My dorm room was above the college radio station and I would hear the bass lines come up through the floor. That inspired me to buy a bass guitar. My roommate played guitar, so we started jamming together."

"My creative process is different every time. I wish there was a formula that I could implement every time I create music so that I always know how to write a good song. Sometimes my inspiration comes from a phrase that I hear on the street or in a conversation and sometimes it comes from a riff I play on guitar. I like to work into the night. The wee hours of the night I find are the most creative time for me. That is when I write most of my songs. Everything that I create I try to make unique to me. I don't try to do what other artists do. I want to do what is uniquely my personality and what is in my heart at that moment."

"There are a lot of things I love about my career as an artist. I love the creative process and the camaraderie that I have with my band and crew. I also love traveling, meeting fans, and writing a song in the morning and being able to play it for an audience that night. But what I love most is having that feeling that I have made a difference. There are moments that I feel this way. Those moments are what make it all worth it for me."

"Over the years, music has given me the strength to get through the challenges in my life. I want my music to do what other music has done for me. I want to help people get through hard times and I want to give them the ability to recognize that those challenges can be something to grow from."

"At every show I play, I hope that people leave feeling transformed from whatever stresses they carried in with them to a place of release. I want them to feel uplifted and positive. When they walk out, I hope they feel inspired to make a difference in the world. I know that sounds like a lot to get from one show, but I feel that at the best concerts I've been to, this is how I have felt afterwards."

"I strive to create conscious music or music that inspires awareness. It could be awareness for an issue, for example, the homeless situation or speaking out against war, singing in support for saving our environment but more than that it is about waking something up in people's hearts so that they open their minds to becoming aware of things that are out there no matter what."

"I hope to awaken the compassion within people to see past obstacles and create a desire inside to reach out and help others. That is the lens I think we need to look through at any issue that is taking place in the world today."

"My partner, Sara Agah, and I started the Do It For The Love Foundation that brings people with advance stages of life-threatening illness, children with severe challenges, and wounded veterans to live concerts. It is like a Make-A-Wish foundation for music. I hope that people who have friends or family members who need music in that way or people that want to volunteer with us will reach out at www.DoItForTheLove.org."

"Music matters to me because . . . it brings out emotions in me that I never knew existed. I want to feel that sense of transformation through music that so many songs and artists have given to me throughout the decades. I want to offer that back to the planet."

Chapter Twenty-One: Chris Funk

Photo Credit: Chris Mueller

Born in Indiana, Chris Funk was surrounded by a music-loving family. His parents encouraged musical exploration. Perhaps because there was so much music, it never really dawned on him to become a musician. It was always inside of him. However, the signs were there. Chris plays countless instruments, among them, the violin, the guitar, the pedal steel, the piano, the saxophone, and the mandolin. He tells the story that he was discovered, but his music speaks for itself. The Decemberists are an edgy, down-to-earth, have-nothing-to-prove kind of band. They can play on NBC's *Parks and Recreation*, or a small pub house in Portland, Oregon. They know what they stand for: it's all about the music.

"Music was always playing around the house and was encouraged from an educational standpoint as well as a creative standpoint in my life. Growing up, my family was very involved in music. My dad was a singer and my mom played the piano. In fact, I don't remember there ever not being some sort of music at my house. Music was always deemed as something valuable. For me it was all about music and bands. I started playing in rock bands on my own in junior high; it was a center of focus for me. It became a huge social avenue for me, too. I started to develop my tribe of people, if you will, in junior high and in high school, from the music that we liked. Music was my focus and obsession."

"Even though it was everything for me, there wasn't a moment when I thought, 'this is it'. I mean, you can say you want to do music for a living, and there are many fields you can take on and jobs you can get in the industry, but you can't say, "I want to make a living doing a band or art". It kind of chooses you when you can make a living doing it. I believe it's not something that you get to pick. I never once felt like this was what I was going to do, even as a kid in high school, playing all this music in symphonic bands, jazz bands, and playing in my rock bands. It never

91

occurred to me that I would do music, which is kind of crazy, with all the educators I had around me and my parents being so supportive. It just took me a while to figure it out."

"I tried to go to college for liberal arts and dropped out because music just kept roping me back in. I started working in the industry of music: working at clubs, trying to get a job on the road to go work sound for a band, or anything I could do to just be on the road and be around it. I think I was kind of fooling myself or just wasn't in touch with myself enough, to know it was what I wanted to do. Then the Decemberists happened and I thought, 'Oh, I'm doing this for a living'. But by that time I was 25 years old. Some people are lucky. They know exactly what they want to do as kids and they do it. I just wasn't one of those people."

"I love playing music. That's it. I can't imagine doing anything else. There have been so many highlights, like playing to help get Barack Obama elected in downtown Portland, and then meeting him. It is one of those moments where you feel like you are doing something with more purpose than just unloading records. It was pretty awesome. There were over 100,000 people who came to that rally, and it was kind of the beginning of Obama's moment in time. I've done some really fun television stuff, too. I got to go on *The Colbert Report* a couple of times and do a really funny guitar duel segment with Steve. Getting to meet your heroes in music, those people you admire or who inspire you, is just the best feeling. I think the highlights come from the musical family and the community you build, and the people you get to meet. Being able to just make records is an honor. There is nothing that I take for granted."

People don't realize that you spend 22 hours a day doing this thing so you can play music for two hours. Being away from your friends and family at the level that we do it at can be challenging, but touring is what everybody wants to do when they are young. It's what people think makes music exciting. Once anything becomes a business, it is a business, whether you want it that way or not. Once you start making your living doing your art, it's like anything else. You're grown up and have responsibilities. We all face those same struggles and challenges. But if you are lucky, you can do what you love."

"I love that people always look to artists for their opinions. I think people forget we are just people. Before the Decemberists happened, I was working as a busboy at a bar. Suddenly you are thrust into the spotlight and you're supposed to have an opinion on world politics. It doesn't always add up, I think, for some people. However, they always say that you have this period in time, right now, where you have the spotlight and you can draw people's attention to things that you become interested in. I think we have the responsibility to form an opinion and become intelligent beings that serve the community, or serve some greater purpose than just selling records."

"There's not just one way to make music. You have to be willing to go on the road and put the time in. But the secret is writing good music that people respond to. Sometimes I can think a song is good all day long. But if no one hears it or gets it and other people don't respond to it, it's still totally fine for me. It served its purpose in me creating something I am satisfied with. The way you get from playing in Laurelhurst at the White Eagle, which is where the Decemberists were playing before we went on the road, to playing in concert halls, takes good music and good fortune. I hope people enjoy the music. I hope it inspires. It is cool that we have been in the band for such a long time that we are starting to meet younger people who tell us the band is the reason they started playing music. It's really one of the most powerful things that you can hear. That's incredible. I hope that our music continues to inspire people."

"Music matters to me because . . . I have no choice."

Chapter Twenty-Two: Christopher "Kiff" Gallagher, Jr.

Christopher "Kiff" Gallagher, Jr., is no stranger to seeing firsthand how business and music can make an impact in communities. Gallagher's impressive résumé includes working for President Clinton, serving as President of Social Venture Network, forming his own record label "Peace Labs Music", and consulting for the Gates Foundation, and Barack Obama. He has been recognized for his outstanding service from organizations such as the Aspen Institute. No wonder, then, that Gallagher has found a unique way to combine his commitment to community service with his love for music in MusicianCorps, a nonprofit organization that trains, teaches, and heals through music.

"Music was and still is a huge part of my life. It is a lifelong passion. Growing up was tough at times for me – my parents didn't always get along, and drama was regular in my home. But we had a music room in our house, and I remember it as a place of comfort. Music-making and listening helped my family feel the love we didn't always know how to show. Some of my favorite childhood memories come from our family time together in that music room."

"As I grew older, music-making was a safe way to explore my emotions, express myself, and learn the creative process. I found that music was the one place I had enough courage to practice, fail, and keep trying. I did this just because I loved it so much."

"I think that MusicianCorps came from a realization that music is an underutilized form of service in our world. I had been a part of the Clinton Campaign in the 1990s, and I was part of the White House's legislative team that created the AmeriCorps program. I wanted to create a Musical Peace Corps because I saw music as a natural gift and strategy to change lives. I wanted to help foster a movement that gave opportunities to all musicians and also provided music as a form of connection. I wanted a place where we could create opportunities to train and support musicians as teachers, mentors, and community care workers. I believe that through music we can transform lives and communities, and so that is what MusicianCorps does."

"The goal of MusicianCorps has always been to put music to work for people, to address critical needs through the power of musical inclusion, and to engage musicians with the right head and heart for it, as community leaders. For me, it comes down to human capital. It's all about valuing music as a form of community capital, and applying music's capacity to help folks transcend barriers in themselves and in their communities."

"There are so many examples of where music has made a difference in people's lives. Think about Gabby Giffords who couldn't speak words, yet learned to sing through music therapy. Think about Steve Jobs who turned Apple around through music. Think about premature babies who thrive when they are treated with music. Think about the seniors who have Alzheimer's disease, but when they hear a favorite song it unlocks memories. These are just a few of the different communities that benefit from music."

"Music is an underutilized tool for the public good. My hope is that the MusicianCorps ethos continues to spread, regardless of our particular organization; we need civic music movement that's bigger than any one approach or locale. Our vision is inclusive. We work with the musicians, the various populations, the schools, hospitals, foster care, seniors, and other communities in so many places. I hope civic and business leaders will work together to leverage the power of music and potential for musicians – beyond commercial entertainment and corporate profit – to reach, teach, and heal in the world."

"The highlights for me have been the personal connections that I see every day, the smiles on faces of children, youth, veterans, seniors and other folks we work with who may have experienced suffering, the musicians who feel a sense of purpose and respect beyond their Facebook and Twitter followers, and the many young people who have developed personally and professionally through the organization."

"Music matters to me because . . . it reminds me that we're all connected and a part of the universe."

Chapter Twenty-Three: Adam Gardner

Photo Credit: Zoe-Ruth Erwin

Adam Gardner cannot imagine a time when music was not his passion. He has been able to incorporate music into his life in two specific ways: Guster and Reverb. Guster is the band he formed with friends during freshman orientation at Tufts. Reverb is the Maine nonprofit that makes touring green, which he founded with his wife, also a Tufts graduate. Reverb has greened 151 tours for bands like Dave Matthews, Maroon 5, and Jack Johnson. Reverb has also reduced 112,276 tons of carbon dioxide in the environment.

"We always had music playing in our house. We had a piano, and I took piano lessons as a kid. It was a huge part of my life. I took trumpet in junior high, and I joined the marching band. I also remember listening to my sister's records in the basement on the stereo for hours. Once I heard The Cars it got me really excited about learning how to play the guitar. As soon as I could play a few chords, I formed a band. I played in that band beginning in 8th grade and through high school. When I graduated from high school and went to college, I met the guys at orientation and we've been a band ever since."

"In the back of my mind, I always wanted music to be a big part of my life. I'm not sure I ever thought of a music career. Music was just my thing. It was what I did. I would come home from soccer practice and go right to band rehearsal. The band we formed was called Gus. We did not think that we were really going to do anything more than be friends who played together in college. We began playing in local clubs, but then we would get asked to open for the national bands passing through Boston. We made a record and sold 50,000 on our own, as Gus. As we grew, it became clear that, for legal reasons, we needed to change our name, because there was a national group that had the same name. We changed our name, but we didn't want to change it too much, so we just added 'ter'."

"We've been a band for 20 years, and, while we've grown musically, the one thing that has been consistent is a strong sense of melody in our songs. We all write together. We usually just start from the point of simply asking, what do we want to say? We play music that makes us happy. If the performers aren't excited about it, then how are we supposed to get our fans interested in it? For me, it is less about a lyrical message and more about the emotional underpinnings of the music we create. What does the song feel like? What is the groove? I find that once the mood is determined, the lyrics follow suit."

"A lot of my world concerns are focused on saving the planet. As I've been touring over so many years, I came to the realization that tours have a huge impact on the environment. My wife and I founded Reverb ten years ago, and have worked with over 150 major tours and reached 18 million fans at concerts."

"Our nonprofit company has two components. The first is to provide tours with green assistance, in order to keep their environmental impact at a minimum. This includes providing waste management, recycling, composting, sourcing local food services, water bottle stations, and catering. Whatever we can do to make a concert more eco-friendly, we do."

"The second part of Reverb is change. As a touring musician, I see the special relationship between bands and their fans. We wanted to harness that relationship to create change. For those bands that work with us, we use their tour as a platform to engage the hundreds and thousands and millions of fans. This has allowed me to relate to other musicians who have nothing to do with my music, but who share a common passion for protecting the environment. We connect with local nonprofit groups, as well as national environmental campaigns, to set up fun programs for fans in eco villages. These programs enhance the concert experience, so fans hopefully take one small action and make a difference. It's not like we are asking people to change their whole universe all at once, just take small steps. We believe many hands turn the wheel."

"Every tour that we have worked with has been great. For me, finding something new that works is always a highlight. We just started a new program with The Dave Matthews band on the Summer 2014 Tour that ties the environment to a social cause. If you think about it, the earth will probably be fine, but what will sustain our lives in a disaster? Farm and Family is one example. We bring together the environment and the social cause through support of local farmers who produce the fresh food we then use to feed people on the tour. This has had a positive impact on communities."

"Music matters to me because . . . it has the power to create change."

Chapter Twenty-Four: Isaac Hanson

Hanson has been a family business for over 20 years. The three brothers from Tulsa, Oklahoma are grown, but they're still singing. Their supportive parents encouraged them musically and they all learned to play piano as young kids. What began as a creative outlet became a phenomenon that included Hanson Day every May 6th and three Grammy nominations. With eight Top 40 albums on the US Billboard 200, the band certainly could have slowed down. Instead they started their own label and created Charity Walks to raise awareness about poverty in the Third World. Hanson approaches the business of music in a refreshingly unique way.

"My parents valued music and artistic expression, so we had plenty of room to explore music growing up. I remember when I was around nine, I asked my mom how to play some chords in the key of C and she showed me C, F, and G. The next thing you know, I wrote what I consider to be my first song."

"We spent many hours watching old movies and listening to oldies radio growing up. There was always music in the house. We loved movies like *Singing in the Rain*. We had a tape that had about 22 hits from 1958, and it was probably the most influential for us. I could remember songs and sing them back, after only hearing them a handful of times. It's still true to this day. I don't have to hear a song very many times before I know almost everything in that song. It is an amazing gift. It's an absolute privilege to have that kind of skill. I honestly will say, though, don't ask me to do that with an algebra problem! Everybody has a unique skill set and design, and I feel lucky that music was the one that I got."

"Music is as much a reflection of culture as it is a mover of the dial, and so music sometimes needs to jumpstart, to encourage, to be something inspiring. There's also room in music to dance and have a good time, to help you get fired up, or to get through a rough breakup. But sometimes, music is there to tell a more complicated story. We believe if you are passionate about something, if you think it's important, it's reasonable and appropriate to say it, and to do it, or do something about it. We have been doing one-mile barefoot charity walks before every show. We sponsor every single person who shows up and walks with us with a dollar donated to one of four causes: either drilling wells, building schools, providing healthcare access and medicine, or promoting shoes in Third World countries."

"The quality of the music we produce, along with the connection to the fans, is our focus. That's what we stand for. We strive to make the best record we can, every single time. We never cranked them out at some silly, fast pace. The music business has changed an extraordinary amount since we started. The business as a whole has been desperately trying to keep selling people plastic CDs, rather than develop artists or find better ways to connect with the audience."

"I see an extraordinary problem in the music business, and Spotify and Pandora can't solve it because it takes 450,000 streams of a song to earn $10.00. You can't make a record for $10.00. It just doesn't work, because it doesn't provide adequate compensation or revenue, for the artists who are writing or performing the songs, to actually create a sustainable business. There has to be a better way to bring the audience into the value of the content that is being made, so that it is a business model that works for all. This is what we think about as artists."

"Music matters to me because . . . it's therapy. It helps me get through the ups and the downs of life."

Chapter Twenty-Five: Beth Harrington

Beth Harrington grew up in Boston, in a home infused with music. Her father encouraged that passion and, once the Beatles rose to fame, Beth was smitten with their music and never looked back. Her films have been widely distributed. In 2003, one of her films was honored with a Grammy nomination. Her latest project, "The Winding Stream", traces the origins of country music, beginning with the Carter-Cash family dynasty. In interviews with Johnny and Rosanne Cash, Janette Carter, and the families that continue their legacy, Beth tells a musical tale.

"I would say the turning point in my life musically was hearing The Beatles for the first time. That just consumed me. They were absolutely my favorite band and they really meant something to me culturally, too. They were more than musicians to me. They represented this other lifestyle that was possible. I became interested in everything that music could do."

"I began making music documentaries to learn more about the people who created cultural music stories. "Welcome to the Club" was about women who were rockabilly singers. They were mainly women from the rural south who came from a country music tradition, and many mentioned the Carter Sisters and Johnny Cash."

"After making this film, I kept thinking that no one had really told the story of how Johnny Cash and the Carter family connected (through his marriage to June Carter, but on a deep musical level as well) and how this one family influenced so many generations of musicians. This was in 2001, but I did not get my idea off the ground really until a few years later."

"The film took over 12 years to make. It was a very long process, because the money to fund these historical projects is not there anymore. Now you have to use things like Kickstarter and grass-root efforts to raise enough money, because the entities that used to grant the money are not in the risk-taking business anymore. It takes longer. I found the whole process to be much more piecemeal, because I had to go back and forth many times to shoot what I needed. Then I would raise a little money and go off and shoot again to round out the story. I would come back, edit that, make a little more money and go off and shoot. It's really an inefficient way to do things, but it's kind of the way things happen now."

"I told the Cash and Carter story without narration. Letting things stand on their own, especially with all the voices in the film already, it seemed we could tell it without a narrator. We felt that it would be better for viewers to follow the material and come to their own conclusions about what they were learning. The film is largely original interview and performance footage we shot, in combination with archival footage and photos and animation. It was a thrill to meet Johnny Cash, as well as the family in Virginia, because he is such an icon, and they carry on the legacy of the Carter music. Getting a chance to sit with the actual people who knew the original Carters, and hear them tell their story was very gratifying. I wanted to replicate that immediacy of experience in the film."

"The origins of American country music are very deep and complex. There is such a great deal of cross-fertilization, from different regions and cultures and places. The Carter family helped synthesize much of that music into one style, which we now call country music. It didn't really have a name then, but they saw that richness and worked with that heritage, and turned it into a big cultural legacy for us. No one put it all together before, because it covers over 80 years of history."

"Making the film was harder than I thought it would be. There were many elements and characters. I think that is one of the reasons we had a hard time getting funding; people couldn't quite understand what we were going for, since there were so many different characters in the story."

"Music matters to me because . . . it fills me up spiritually and connects me with every other human being. I think all people respond to music. Even if you don't share a common language, music cuts across languages and cultures and other barriers. I think reaching across all those barriers is one of the most powerful things on the planet."

Chapter Twenty-Six: Kent Hartman

It took Kent Hartman 48 years to realize he had a talent for writing about his passion: music. Music was always around him. He worked in the industry as a tour merchandiser and in marketing, he owned a rock and roll café, and he even produced a nationally-syndicated radio show. How appropriate that his story, *The Wrecking Crew*, was about the back-up instrumentalists of the 1960s and 1970s who played in place of big names like The Beach Boys, The Byrds, and The Mamas and the Papas in the studio on those artists' own records. The book became a national bestseller and will be both a feature film and a Broadway show.

"Music played a large role in my life as a kid. When I was four years old, my parents enrolled me in a preschool called Mrs. Rooney's Musical Kindercollege. This was way back in the early 1960s. I went there daily and it was all just about music every day. I don't know how my mother found out about the Kindercollege, but I loved it. I'm not sure why she picked that school. Maybe because she thought it would be fun for me or maybe because I had already shown musical interest, but that school is really where my love for music started. I was just crazy about music and have been ever since."

"I think my story is different from most. I wasn't one of those people who grew up knowing that writing was what I wanted to do. In fact, it never entered my head. I was somebody who spent all of my 20s in education. I went to college and then to law school for a couple of years. I also got a Master's degree in international relations and then I got an MBA. So all I did was school stuff in my 20s. When I was 30 or 31, I moved to L.A. and worked as a financial aid director at a college, but I was always trying to figure out how to get into the music business. I eventually became a music industry entrepreneur and worked with dozens of well-known artists, like Steppenwolf, Counting Crows, and Lyle Lovett. I spent 20 years doing that, and then I wrote the book."

"It was only about six years ago, when I was 48, that I found this other passion. I had worked in the music business for a long time. Over the years I'd heard many great, behind-the-scenes stories about a group of people in the music business that no one really knew much about. This group was called The Wrecking Crew. I had gotten to know a couple of The Wrecking Crew guys a long time ago. They would tell me stories about their careers and how they did the work in the studios for so many famous musicians. My girlfriend suggested that I put together an article and submit it to American Heritage magazine as one of their big feature stories. I pitched it to them and they went for it. My writing career really happened from that point on. I wrote a well-received article called 'The Wrecking Crew'" and then a literary agent contacted me – a bunch of agents, actually – and I signed with one of them. After subsequently inking a deal with a major publisher, I then wrote the book and now the screenplay, too."

"It has been eye-opening because, though the producers in Hollywood optioned my book a year or two ago, they had a really tough time figuring out how to write the screenplay. If you read my book, you don't automatically read it and think, 'Oh, I see what the movie would be here'. There are so many characters in my book and they needed to be narrowed down for a movie. The producers finally asked me to write the screenplay, even though I had never written one before. I thought, I have never written a book before either, so how hard can it be? So I wrote the screenplay, and, for whatever reason, they loved it and are moving forward with the movie."

"I've learned from all of this that you've really just got to have confidence. Like Malcolm Gladwell said, you have to put in your 10,000 hours of time into whatever it is you want to be a super-success at. If you put in 10,000 hours of time relating to that dream, by the time you get to the $10,000^{th}$ hour, you are going to be pretty darn good. For me it has been kind of a growing process. The challenge in writing a decent book is that you have to do in-depth research. Leave no stone unturned, because it's always the one interview that you almost didn't do that ends up being the best. That's one of the things I've learned in my writing. The other is that you have to be able to sit in one place and concentrate for great lengths of time. Not just when you are writing, but for six months or a year, or whatever it is going to take to write the text."

"I would say I am probably atypical compared to most other writers. I am not a morning person. I have always very much been a night person, so when I wrote *The Wrecking Crew* I would say 80 percent of it was written after 11 o'clock at night. I would routinely go to bed at three or four in the morning, then wake up at 10 or 11 in the morning, go about my day and do various things, and then I would settle down for another evening of writing. So I almost always write at night. I rarely write during the day. That just works for me. I have a friend who is also an author and he has a very specific schedule. At 6 a.m. he's up, and by 7:30 a.m. he's at his desk and writes until like noon or 1:00 p. m. That's his routine every day because his ideas happen in the morning."

"I hope readers take away from my stories the feeling of being there. With *The Wrecking Crew*, I want them to feel like they are right there in the recording studio. Whenever I write, I want the reader to feel like they are able to experience the smell and the sound and the touch and the taste; all those senses. This is what I hope I convey when I write."

"Music matters to me because . . . it is who I am."

Chapter Twenty-Seven: Russel Hornbeek

Russel Hornbeek grew up knowing his path, and that path was music. Music Saves Lives began in 2005 with a simple concept: use the music and entertainment industry to motivate youth to donate blood and register for the bone marrow database. This nonprofit sprung from a personal tragedy, but has transformed thousands of lives. In less time than it takes to see a movie, a life can be saved. Russel has seen it happen first-hand.

"I have always loved music. But more than that, I've always loved sharing music. Even in junior high and high school, I was setting up bands to play at other schools. Organizing different music events was a connection for me. I love all kinds of music, but rock/alternative is my choice. I grew up with U2, The Police, Led Zeppelin, and Steely Dan, and then I just graduated into Nirvana and Pearl Jam; then the Foo Fighters. I have always stayed connected to that alternative world of music."

"I went to private school. I went to Christian schools when I was younger, and the one thing that I was always taught was to be a leader. I enjoyed being the boss and making things happen. I think my education from an early age all the way up taught me that you've got to take that leap of faith and do it, and not just be someone who tags along and looks at what somebody else does. You have to make a difference in the world and do it yourself."

"I graduated from high school, got married early, and started a business in the medical field. That business is what tied everything together. While working in the medical field for 17 years, I saw how music helped people. Music is everywhere. Everybody listens to it in one form or another, from their cars to waking up in the morning. Music Saves Lives is all about how music really soothes people."

"Another experience that inspired me was seeing my cousin battle cancer at 16 years old. He needed a lot of blood after his cancer treatments. It hit me hard. It became part of my life. I wondered, 'Where does all the blood that's needed come from and how are we going to make sure it's there in case somebody else needs it?' I spent time thinking about how it would work and then focused on making it happen. I didn't just talk about it. I made it my goal to start this organization. I realized that every part of Music Saves Lives was positive. If I work with a band and they want to help me promote the cause, it's great and it's good for them because they get promotion with their music. If we go out and we encourage somebody to donate blood, then it saves lives. I wake up every morning now thinking, 'Wow, I have one of the most perfect jobs in the whole world'. I feel it's perfect because it's purely positive in every way."

"One of the things that I like doing with Music Saves Lives is finding bands that are up and coming and new to the industry. Being able to talk to those band members while still young and unsigned to a label is pivotal, so that they are supportive of Music Saves Lives when they make it big and have a song that climbs the radio charts. There have been bands and artists I still keep in contact with, like Tom Higgenson, of The Plain White T's. We connected way before he had a hit with 'Hey There Delilah'."

"Music matters to me because . . . I'm doing everything I can to save lives through music. Music connects the world together. It connects life. Saving lives never sounded so good."

Chapter Twenty-Eight: Rosalie Howarth

As an emancipated minor, Rosalie Howarth explored the explosion of music in the 1960s on her own terms. Growing up in Monterey, California, she gained a first-hand education by watching aspiring musicians who would later become legends. She never forgot the musical passion they inspired in her as a child. A popular and respected radio host, Rosalie has been a San Francisco radio personality for over 30 years. She hosts and produces KFOG's *Acoustic Sunrise* and *Acoustic Sunset*, both in their 20th year. Like the legends she watched from the rooftops, Rosalie is a radio legend, inducted into the Bay Area Radio Hall of Fame in 2011.

"As a kid, I hung out at a coffeehouse in Monterey every chance I got. This was decades before the term *barista* was even invented. In coffeehouses those days, people went to drink coffee, debate ideas, or recite poetry. It was a venue for public discussion. There was always somebody playing an acoustic guitar in the corner. An English teacher there turned me on to Bob Dylan. I will forever thank him for that. My early introduction to Dylan's music made my life take a little bit of a left turn."

"Starting in 1967, the so-called Summer of Love, I began running away to the Haight-Ashbury. I would come back after a few weeks, and, though my parents were beside themselves at the time, they agreed to give me an emancipated minor document when I proved I would keep my grades up by getting straight As. I was really, really young. It all looked glamorous and full of flower-power to me. I failed to see the seamy underside and was very fortunate to come out of some of those experiences completely unscathed."

"I loved sneaking into the Monterey Pop Festival. Being very nimble, I climbed up the back of some of the horse corrals that lined the side of the arena. Lying on a rooftop of a stable hour after hour, I watched The Who, Janis Joplin, and Jimi Hendrix. I remember people being freaked out by Hendrix. It's all so historical now, but at the time, he was reviled for the violence and the sexual innuendo with the guitar, because this was a pop festival. Those experiences definitely filled me with the thrilling sounds of what kind of an alternate universe there could be with that type of music."

"In the early 1970s, I started working at a record store, because that was how you could get close to the music. You got to listen all day, and see and hear the new LPs as your favorite artists released them. This was a key element of opening my eyes and ears to music. The music I favor today and play on my program is largely acoustic-based. It's what David Crosby used to call, 'wooden music'. I think when you strip out the amplification and props that bands can lean on, you're left with the person, the instrument, and the words. That purity allows you to truly appreciate those experiences. We have become so niched! Every radio station is devoted to just one genre. I wish everybody in America could have access to a wide-ranging radio station that played different genres of music. There is no chance that you might blunder in and discover you love bluegrass if you only listen to a hip-hop station."

"Music matters to me because . . . it can provide tremendous comfort. Knowing that you're not the only one to have felt these emotions joins us together. Music makes us feel more of the cosmic unity that I think, without knowing it, we all yearn for."

Chapter Twenty-Nine: Luke Jerram

Photo Credit: Luke Jerram

Luke Jerram had wide-open spaces to explore, growing up in a small country village north of Bristol. As a young boy, Luke used nature as his tools, and found endless possibilities in building sculpture with stones, drawing with sticks, or painting on leaves. With talent to pursue many careers, his parents encouraged him to test his abilities. Luke studied math, physics, and art, all at A-level. He earned a place to study engineering at university, but the strong pull to pursue the more risky path of art never left him. He gave up his spot and has never looked back. In fact, he prefers to look outside the box, always questioning perception in his large-scale performance pieces. From his "Sky Orchestra" hot air balloons wired with sound that float over the earth while playing original compositions, to his "Play Me I'm Yours" pianos that are left on the streets for pedestrians to play, Luke pushes the boundaries between what is considered music and what is art.

"I'm very interested in learning how things work. There's a part of my brain that's programmed to think about how to make things and how take things apart, like an engineer. Many of my art projects involve engineering science and perception. I was always interested in making things as a young child, and later as a student. When I was in university, education was free, which was amazing. I could take the risk for art. Now in the UK, we've moved to an American system where you have to pay more than £10,000 pounds a year to study. Coming out of college with such large debts, I really wouldn't have been able to study art. I would have probably completed the engineering degree instead. I imagine I'd be designing new razor products for Gillette by now!"

"I was really lucky in school. I had a university tutor who inspired me, and I chose to pursue art. I received practical advice: 'Keep up your stamina and follow through, ignore the dissatisfaction of others, don't put up with rubbish, and always make the best art you can'. We'd talk about all of those rules, about breaking them, and making things as extreme as possible. If it's going to be big, make it really big. If it's going to be beautiful, make it really beautiful. If it's going to be quiet and boring, make it really quiet and boring. There is something quite truthful about that, because in today's society, we as artists are compelled to make things, but we have to compete with TV and the Internet. I guess that is part of why I choose to do the live art projects. It's always a bit of a risk, but it's always dramatic."

"Sometimes my inspiration for these musical pieces comes from other ideas that don't work the first time I try them. The idea for 'Play Me I'm Yours', where we put decorated pianos in public areas for people to play, came out of a Sky Orchestra failure that happened in 2007. We tried to fly hot air balloons over Birmingham with the Birmingham symphony orchestra in the hot air balloons. We all turned up to fly very early in the morning, but it was too windy. We couldn't go up in the balloons, but we still had to pay all of the musicians at music union rates and all the balloon pilots for showing up. Suddenly we'd spent £15,000 and had no artwork to show for it. We'd promised the city council of Birmingham that we'd reach 100,000 people across the city with this large-scale artwork, and we had delivered nothing. We had a little bit of money left, and used it to deliver the street piano project. With 15 pianos placed on streets across the city for the public to play, we ended up reaching 140,000 people in Birmingham and the project was a great success. The project has been more successful in some respects than the Sky Orchestra, because I've now presented it to more than 45 cities worldwide."

"I love it when my art takes flight to new realms. I create a piece of artwork and it seems to find its own audience in the world. If you make a glass sculpture, it fits and works in the context of museums and galleries, whereas the piano project has been presented in city-wide music festivals, live art festivals, and piano competitions. It works in different ways. The piano is good for those who don't have access to pianos to play. The pianos reach audiences who wouldn't go into a gallery or museum. We are delivering a piano to their neighborhood for the community to enjoy. It's also about getting people together to cross social barriers. The pianos provide a blank canvas for the public's creativity. When I make an artwork, I don't worry about where it will end up. Each artistic project finds its own audience, as well as context for presentation. Some artwork tours for years, while others only get presented once. When we presented the 'Play Me I'm Yours' installation in Boston in October 2013, for example, we reached number 1000. It is very exciting that my street piano projects have been shown 1000 times in different places around the world. It is remarkable to me that this project has found an audience that exceeds eight million people."

"Music matters to me because . . . it's the oxygen in my blood."

Chapter Thirty: Dr. Costas Karageorghis

Dr. Costas Karageorghis is a reader in sport psychology at Brunel University, London, and author of the popular text *Inside Sport Psychology*. He is the world's leading expert on the psychology of music in the domain of exercise and sport. His research has revealed many different ways in which music can enhance performance in this domain. His studies are regularly featured in newspapers around the world: most recently in the *Times, Independent, New York Times, Wall Street Journal,* and *Washington Post*. Among the several awards and honors he has received, in 2011 he was awarded the coveted Sportesse Award for Exercise Sciences (UK) for his theoretical work in the area of music and physical activity. He has contributed to many album projects in his career, and recently collaborated with leading British soprano Laura Wright on *The Sound of Strength* (Decca Records), which is the first classical music album to be written and arranged specifically for physical exercise.

"When I was a youngster, music was all around me—and many difference types of music that represented all corners of the globe—but it was certainly not portable! Now with the advent of the iPod, and other personal listening devices, it is relatively easy to create your own listening bubble. People can often be seen becoming lost in music as a consequence of the technologies that are now readily available. Music is an integral part of human socialization. Many people form social cliques and hold social identities, through their style of dress for example, that are directly related to the type of music that they listen to. Also, most people use music as part of a mood regulation strategy on a daily basis. I think with the advent of new technology, music has become even more pervasive, especially among young people."

"I grew up above a second-hand record store in South London in quite a socially-deprived neighborhood. Every morning I would be awakened by the thumping bass frequencies from the store below that literally made the floor boards rattle. I would look out of my bedroom window at passers-by and notice how, as they came within earshot of the music, their facial expressions would change; their faces would lift. The music would also put a distinct bounce in their step. The music from that store provided the auditory background for every single activity in the neighborhood: panhandling, hustling, wheeling and dealing, you name it. From that tender age I became very interested in the psychological effects of music but also got heavily involved in track and field. I went on to study for a BS in sports science and music at university. Fortunately, my lecturers allowed me to merge these two areas during my final year and that's when I conducted my first formal investigation into the effects of music on physical activity."

"In the study into the effects of music on physical activity, we consider the influence of a range of music factors. For example, the melody, harmony, rhythmic qualities, and lyrical content are essential elements of the musical stimulus. The way in which the stimulus takes effect is influenced by a range of personal factors such as one's age, social-cultural upbringing, gender, attentional style, and training status. Situational or context-related factors influence a number of outcomes. These outcomes can be psychological in nature, such as your mood or affective state. They can be psychophysical, such as how hard you think you're working. They can be psychophysiological, so the music might affect your blood pressure, heart rate, and galvanic skin response. They might be behavioral in nature and, for example, music can influence how much effort you expend in a given activity."

"As you can see, this interaction of music factors, personal factors, and situational factors have a strong bearing on the consequences associated with music use. There is also an appraisal process that takes place once you have used music in a sport or physical activity content. The appraisal of how effective the music is influences your future selection decisions. So there is a feedback loop from the outcomes, back into the music factors, in terms of what you select as an accompaniment for future activities."

"The motivational qualities of music relate to four main causal factors. These causal factors are both internal and external in nature. The internal factors pertain to the musical stimulus itself and the external factors pertain to how an individual interprets a given piece of music. The internal factors are rhythm response, which has to do with the rhythmical qualities of music and musicality, the combination of harmony and melody. The external factors are cultural impact, and this concerns how culturally pervasive a given piece of music is and how likely you are to have been exposed to it. The more we are exposed to pieces of music, the more we develop the liking for them; however it's an inverted-U type relationship so over-exposure can lead to the disliking of a given piece. The final factor is extra-musical association, and this is where we link music to a particular film, video, TV show, or even a life experience. Perhaps the music conjures heroic images or images associated with overcoming adversity. It can make us feel more motivated purely through association (e.g., hearing 'Gonna Fly Now' by Bill Conti conjures images of Rocky Balboa's heroic feats in the *Rocky* film series). Collectively, these factors account for the motivational quotient of a piece of music, which impacts on the outcomes that I described earlier, such as positive mood responses, reductions in perceived exertion, and a range of behavioral consequences."

"When I devise playlists for training, I look at the interaction of the individual, the nature of the activity in which they are engaged, the intensity of their activity, and what their personal goals are. As a starting point, I would interview an individual and maybe administer some psychometric instruments. I might, for example, ascertain what their optimal mood is pre-competition, so that I can match music to that particular type of mood. I get them to bring me their music library. We would discuss it, assess it, and then I would look at a range of factors that pertain to which music is likely to optimize their pre-competition mindset."

"There are many factors to consider. It might be that they have an affiliation or affinity with a particular artist. I would look at the rhythmical qualities of the music, particularly if they are matching it to a psych-up routine. Often athletes don't want to burn off too much psychological energy pre-competition, so the tempo, which often determines how stimulating a piece of music is, will be a critical factor. I would look at the harmony of the music. Say they want to feel happy for example, I might use pieces of music that are characterized by predominantly major harmonies. I would look at the lyrical content of the music and search for an affirmation that might enhance their confidence or resolve, such as 'search for the hero inside of you'. Sometimes it might be an activity-related affirmation, such as 'run to the beat', 'work your body', 'let's get physical', 'play hard' and so on."

"I often look very carefully at lyrics and match them to specific types of activity. I would also try to arrange the playlist in such a way that the mood is modulated towards an optimal state just before competition. If it's a training session I am creating the playlist for, I would often set the tempo of the playlist to contour the expected heart-rate of the workout.

"Within the workout, I would segment the music content very carefully into pre-workout mental preparation: a warm up, cardiovascular activity, anaerobic activity such as resistance training or plyometric training, followed by warm-down related activities and the stretching component right at the end. I would try to find tracks that match the nature of each segment of the activity and the preferences of the individual or group involved. In so doing, I would hope to optimize the playlist for the benefit of the athletes or exercisers."

"Music selection is a very personal thing. I often reiterate what Lucretius the great Roman philosopher said 'One man's meat is another man's poison' or to use modern-day parlance, 'One person's music is another person's noise'. It's not a case of one-size-fits-all when it comes to music. You must consider an individual's characteristics, the nature of the task, the intensity of the task and their desired outcomes. If you marry these factors, your music selection is likely to be optimized. I would hasten to add that music is not for all athletes and exercisers. Some people have what we term an 'associative attentional style', which means they have a tendency to focus inwardly, on regulating the technical aspects of their performance, regulating their heart rate, muscular tension, and so on. For these types of people, music can often be an unwanted distraction."

"I remember very early in my career, I interviewed the double gold-medal winning decathlete and world-record holder Daley Thompson (Great Britain). He won two gold medals in successive Olympic Games: Moscow, 1980 and L.A., 1984. I asked him about his music use during training, and he told me that music was an anathema to him. He was so intent on listening to his body that he did not need external stimulation such as music. This finding has been reiterated in my research across many athletes who have this inward, or associative–type, focus, so music is not for everybody and there are limitations to its use in the realm of sport and physical activity. Nonetheless, for people who choose to use music, taking into account the factors that I have expounded, will likely maximize their enjoyment and the benefits that they will derive."

"Music matters to me because . . . if I think from my own perspective as a scientist and as a musician, it is one of those activities that gives life meaning and truly makes it worth living. Music enriches every day of my existence. It provides a soundtrack to my life and enables me to look forward to a whole range of activities such as moving in time to music, listening to music with significant others in my life, and making music with my jazz trio. All of these things are hugely important to me."

Chapter Thirty-One: Chaka Khan

Chaka Khan, the 10-time Grammy Award winner, has a résumé that spans over 40 years. She has worked with legends from Dizzy Gillespie and Stevie Wonder to Eric Clapton, Gladys Knight, and Prince. Growing up in a supportive and musical home in Chicago, she listened to a wide variety of genres. This exposure instilled in her a love for singing and, remarkably, she can sing in almost any genre. From an early age, her talent was clear. Her 22-album career began as an 18-year-old lead singer in the 1970s with the band, Rufus. She has a star on the Hollywood Walk of Fame and close to 1.7 million Facebook followers. In 2013, her hometown named a street after her and declared it "Chaka Khan Day" on July 28. She is a writer, activist, and founder of the Chaka Khan Foundation. Even with all the accolades and awards and commitments, she remains humble, true to herself, and her music conveys that sensitivity.

"I grew up listening to my parents' music. They were avid music fans. My parents were artists themselves, so they were very creative. They liked all the genres, from opera to jazz, so I got to hear everything. But I mostly listened to my father's music, which was lots and lots of jazz. I can truly say that I grew up on jazz music. I just loved that sound."

"I absolutely didn't think I would become a singer. In fact, when I was young, I went to a catholic school, so I wanted to be a nun. And then I wanted to be a teacher. And then as I got older I wanted to be an anthropologist. And now I'm a singer! There wasn't a true 'ah ha moment' when it dawned on me that I could become a professional singer. But what did come to mind was 'wow I can do this!' and that happened because I did a lot of talent shows growing up."

"I was lucky because my parents were really supportive of my art. I remember my mother used to take my sister and me and the other girls to different talent shows around Illinois. I'd formed a singing group called the Crystalettes. We had a lot of fun. We'd get our outfits, and do our makeup, and our hair, and we'd win a lot of those talent shows. People used to throw money on the stage after my singing performances and I think at that point I realized 'Hey, this is pretty cool and I know I can really do this'."

"When I sing, it's like a spiritual cleansing for me. It's the way that I meditate. I just want to put out there what I'm thinking and what I'm feeling in the most pure form. My creative process really depends on the project that I'm working on. I don't think I have one process that I use all the time. For example, my next project will be a tribute to Joni Mitchell. This is something I've wanted to do for years. I'm going in the studio very soon to start that project. It will be a lot of fun because I love Joni Mitchell. But in order to do the tribute I'm going to be thinking very differently when I do that. I want to be really careful with it because it's singing someone else's material. My goal is to get it done and make it as good as I possibly can."

"I have worked with so many wonderfully talented people. I would have to say that one highlight in my life was working with Arif Mardin. He was one of my musical mentors. He was also like an uncle to me. He was such a great man. He challenged me musically. I think it's a powerful thing when a mentor can do that. To be challenged in your art by another person you trust allows you to grow. Another highlight has to be recording and performing with the jazz greats Dizzy Gillespie and Miles Davis, because these were the people I grew up listening to. Working with each of them was inspiring and life-changing."

"I think music is necessary for living. Musicians and artists are the dreamers in society. Without these dreamers in society there would be nothing. Many students in schools right now don't have the opportunity to have music and that's really going to affect them. That's troubling to me. It's that creative right-brain that needs to be nurtured and developed because it's a very powerful thing."

"I find my inspirations in everyday life. When you think about it, there's a lot going on in just everyday life. I learn from the people I'm around and that I know. I stay balanced with everything that I do by the grace of God and by following my heart. I work hard to accomplish everything that I want to do and I stick to it and everything seems to work out. I love to sing, and singing for people brings me joy. It's why I do what I do."

"Music matters to me because . . . it's my therapy."

Chapter Thirty-Two: Gregory Kozak

Gregory Kozak's first brush with music happened in high school. He had never played an instrument, and lacked training in melody, but he desperately wanted to join the school band. He was assigned to the rhythm section at the very back of the orchestra. Working the bass drum and learning about sounds made an indelible impact. From that first pounding smash of the mallet, he found his passion. Over the next several years, he spent his time playing music, reading about music, and learning music from a wide variety of teachers. A circuitous path through improvisational, classical, jazz, and musical traditions from around the world led to an abiding fascination with the look and sound of musical instruments and performance . . . and, in 1998, Scrap Arts Music was born. Using materials collected in and around his home base of Vancouver, Canada, he invents, designs, and builds instruments like Plankophones, Scorpion Drums, and Bagoleons. In original performance-based work, his company demonstrates that music really can be made from anything.

"My neurons are patterned to be musical. I have a compelling urge to make my own instruments. I've had that urge since I was a teen, so Scrap Arts Music came about very intentionally. I wanted to create an orchestra of my own devising. I also wanted to write all my own music, and design my own choreography. This was the challenge I set for myself. I went back to school to study welding. I taught myself orchestration. I studied all day, every day."

"It was very important to me to reinvent the concept of the instrument. I use recycled materials because I want to make them live again. I make reeds out of Home Depot shopping bags. I make wind instruments out of sailboard masts. I make stringed instruments out of sawmill carts. I make instruments out of debris. I use recycled materials to challenge the concept of what is considered trash. I believe we have two powers here on Earth: to make things or to destroy things. I choose to make things out of what people throw away."

"I want people to create music and give consideration to new ways of performing with musical instruments. My instruments are unique, but anybody with discipline and focus can create one. I'd love to have more people doing this! Every city should have its own orchestra of invented instruments, making original, incredible, and unique music. It would be totally amazing."

"Music makes people imagine. It creates a sense of togetherness through sound. It is an act of creativity that's so positive. We can play music by ourselves, with others, at any age, in any culture. It's such a great moderator of the human experience. I hope people are inspired to look at the world a little differently after seeing and hearing my instruments."

"Music matters to me because . . . it's like food and it's like love. What else is there? At this point in my life, it's the blood in my veins, and the air that I breathe."

Chapter Thirty-Three: Bernie Krause

Bernie Krause believes animals taught us to dance and sing. A pioneer in the field of soundscape ecology, he studies the collective natural voices of habitats – biophonics – and links those observations to the primal inspiration of human choruses and orchestras. As a soundscape recordist, he has studied the planet's sounds that often go unnoticed, such as the multiple ways in which the wind in the leaves, the flutter of hummingbird wings, singing ants, and the howls of wolves all miraculously find acoustic and temporal bandwidth and somehow coalesce. In other words, he had found the origins of human music in the world's wild places. By his fourth year, Bernie's musical life had already begun with the study of classical violin and composition. He experimented with a wide variety of instruments including the cello, viola, violin, and banjo, before settling on guitar. With his late music partner, Paul Beaver, Bernie introduced the synthesizer to pop music and film on the West Coast. He is also the first musician to incorporate natural soundscapes as the core component of his compositions, and has performed with some of the most important names in music. Recently, in collaboration with Oxford composer-in-residence, Richard Blackford, he composed the first symphonic piece inspired largely from whole biophonics. Based on the premise of a recent book by the same title, the commissioned piece, titled *The Great Animal Orchestra: Symphony for Orchestra and Wild Soundscapes*, premiered on the 12th of July, 2014, at the Cheltenham Music Festival in the UK, with the 70-piece BBC National Orchestra of Wales performing and Martyn Brabbins conducting. The team has been commissioned by Alonzo King's LINES Ballet, a major San Francisco performance group, to also write the score for a dance piece that premieres in April, 2015.

"Growing up in Detroit, sound was my window to the world because I don't see very well. So my experience of life has mostly been informed by what I hear. Also, I suffered from a pretty bad case of ADHD and dyslexia from the time I was a kid to well into my adult years; playing music and, later, listening to natural soundscapes helped mitigate the extremes of the disorder. Although my family wasn't at all musical, I was drawn to the sound of the violin before my fourth birthday. When I turned 13, the hormones kicked in and I switched to guitar, becoming a student of many styles including jazz, classical, and what was considered pop in the mid-1950s."

"To pick up a bit of extra spending money during my undergraduate days at the University of Michigan, I played and sang folk music, occasionally working as a studio musician for early Motown recording sessions. For $5.00 a night, I would drive into Detroit for evening sessions, and then head back in the early morning hours for classes. After graduation, I moved east to the Boston area to study communications, working part-time at a local concert booking agency that promoted folk acts such as Joan Baez, Lightning Hopkins, Flatt & Scruggs, Jesse Fuller, and Sonny Terry & Brownie McGee. For one event, we booked The Weavers to perform locally, and word got out that they were looking for a replacement for Frank Hamilton, who occupied what was known as 'the Pete Seeger slot'. Having won the audition, I joined the group in May, 1963 at their Carnegie Hall reunion concerts."

"After the group disbanded in early 1964, I moved to California to study electronic music at Mills College. While there, an acquaintance introduced me to Paul Beaver, an L.A. studio musician. Together we formed a team – Beaver & Krause – and bought one of the first Moog synthesizers off the line. Our work can be heard on over 135 film scores like *Apocalypse Now*, *Rosemary's Baby*, and *Performance*, plus numerous contributions to albums for The Byrds, The Doors, Van Morrison, George

Harrison, Mick Jagger, Carly Simon, Barbra Streisand, and The Monkees, not to mention our own charted music."

"My transition from performing and making music to recording natural soundscapes happened purely by accident. Our first album for Warner Brothers was titled 'In a Wild Sanctuary'. Historically, it was the first LP to feature the theme of ecology and also the first to incorporate natural soundscapes as integral textures of the composition. The production meant that one of us had to venture from the safety of the studio into the uncertainties of the natural world to get the sounds we needed. Paul, more terrified and reluctant than me, handed me a small portable recorder and a stereo set of mics and wished me luck."

"Muir Woods is a small urban park located in a stand of redwoods just north of San Francisco. It comes replete with well-marked paths, lots of signage, rangers eager to explain the spawning habits of migrating salmon, and gift shops – you know, the typical American version of the managed wild. For my first venture into what I thought was 'wild', I picked that spot to record because it was close by and I'd accept whatever wildlife sounds I could get. Of course, never having spent much time outside, I didn't realize that it was fall, a time when most of the birds had already fledged and migrated, so there was little birdsong left to be heard, let alone record. But when I turned on the recorder and heard the hushed ambience in my earphones, mixed with a few ravens, a distant pileated woodpecker's call, and a flock of migrating geese flying high overhead – the sound was so captivating and engaging that it was an epiphany for me. For the first time, listening to natural soundscapes, I felt calmed and not distracted. At that moment, I decided that those were the kinds of environments I would strive to engage with for the rest of my working life. I also realized that the connection to music was immediate – the perfect brainstorm."

"One of the first musical puzzles was the question that if birds are so musical how is it that of the nearly 10,000 bird species worldwide, fewer than a hundred have been incorporated into western music? Repeatedly, when trying to connect nature and music, we composers made the reductive gaffe of ascribing musicality only to those animal vocalizations that happened to fit the musical paradigms we considered melodious. Many bird vocalizations are so complex that they are all but impossible to notate in detail. But that limitation is not restricted to birds. Think of the scant number of signature animals we've incorporated or celebrated in our so-called nature-related music; certain whales (humpbacks mostly), wolves, and a few birds. And Messiaen, the mid-20th century French avant-garde composer used as examples a large percentage of the birds that have been represented. I was always curious why frogs, rhinos, cheetahs, or sea anemones were not considered musical enough to enjoy a place in our palette of compositional expressions. Until now, why haven't composers included whole natural soundscapes as orchestral textures? Come to think of it, following the fragmented models of the biological sciences, most western composers have adopted the concept of single animal voices into their music as abstract and deconstructed expressions. This approach confirms the profound cultural disconnect that exists between many composers and their sense of the living, natural world around them. It is no accident that many of these musical products have become the ultimate expression of that disparity."

"My archive consists of over 5,000 hours of natural soundscapes – marine and terrestrial. These are whole habitat recordings collected worldwide. Within that collection are more than 15,000 identified species. Sadly, 50% of that collection comes from habitats so radically altered, mostly by human intervention, that they are either altogether silent, or their unique collective voices can no longer be heard in any form. That loss has occurred over the period of just 47 years in the field. Of course, there are many more lessons to be learned from natural soundscapes. In order to hear them, we will need to preserve what's left and stop imposing our incessant and often destructive human acoustic signatures (noise) on this otherwise lovely sounding fabric of the wild natural."

"Music matters to me because . . . it defines our place in this world in relation to all of its other sonic components. In particular, and at the moment, it eloquently describes our incoherent and fractured sense of the living world around us and bears little relationship to its divine origins. And the question for us remains: Is that important?"

Chapter Thirty-Four: Patrick Laird

Break of Reality is a unique band. Since forming in 2003, this band has approached the business of music with a new purpose. A rock quartet that uses classical instruments, Break of Reality is organically composed, yet socially sophisticated. They know how to use Kickstarter to fund the tours, they independently release their albums, and know what it takes to promote their music on social media. Best of all, they know how to give back. Their goal is to increase music awareness, not their bottom line. Each show stops at a public school in the area, where the musicians work with students who need music the most. They have captured the hearts of many.

"Music pretty much consumed my life as a kid, and I never looked back. I started playing the cello when I was 10 years old, and my father always pushed me to practice a lot. I didn't always like practicing, but early on, the cello became a major part of my life. As I went through high school, I was exposed to all types of music. My school had a thriving band and chorus program, so I joined both. I learned to play many different instruments in the school band, mainly the bassoon and percussion. My metal-head friends would take me to concerts to see bands like Slayer and Metallica. Between practicing cello, studying classical music, playing in local symphonies, taking up choir and band, and going to see rock concerts, my life was dominated by music."

"The band grew up in supportive public school music programs, so working with kids has always been something that we've felt compelled to do. About a year ago, we came up with the idea of creating a tour that would bring us to schools around the country, providing free workshops and concerts in each district. However, going on tour for a month is still an expensive endeavor, so we figured we'd jump on the Kickstarter bandwagon and raise the money from our fans and supporters. We were

146

overwhelmed by the support from our fans, raising over $50,000 to make the tour happen. Because the tour expenses are covered by our fans, we're able to give 100% of the ticket and donation proceeds from the school concerts to each school's music program."

"Our goal is to inspire music students and teach them to think outside of the box, using their instruments. We aim to raise awareness and funding for music education. We give these educational workshops because music students always come away inspired to write, arrange, practice, and perform more music. Students who are interested in pursuing a career in music are especially interested in what it takes to become a professional musician. Students need to be exposed to professional music groups to get inspired. We continue to get positive feedback from music directors about our workshops, and often we hear that the number of cello students has doubled since our visit!"

"Music matters to me because . . . it's an outlet to express what I feel. It's a language that knows no borders. I love that I can play music anywhere in the world and it can have an emotional effect on people, regardless of where they're from or what language they speak."

Chapter Thirty-Five: Storm Large

Photo Credit: Laura Domela

Storm Large: her name conjures up boldness, an outpouring of compelling emotion, drama, and vibrant activity. She's an actor, author, and playwright. She's even been a reality star who made it to the second to last show of *Rockstar Supernova* in 2006. But most of all she's a singer who found her gifted voice at the young age of five and hasn't stopped singing.

"Music always held hope for me. No matter how angry or rough the sound or message, it spoke of a place and people living and doing something else, somewhere else. It asked, demanded, and answered freedom, with so many voices. Like a city I knew I needed to go to. Not so much escape, more a homing signal."

"I always knew I could sing, but never in a million years would I have guessed I WOULD. For real. In a band. For a short time in the early 1990s in SF, I was a heroin addict. During that time, a friend of mine asked if I would sing one song with his band. The song was Pat Benatar's 'Heartbreaker'. The moment I finished, the place went berserk and several people approached me and asked if I would sing for their bands. That was 23 years ago."

"Throughout that time there have been many highlights but highlight number one is that I get to sing for a living. And that is CRAZY. The 'crazy' was highlight number two: My Carnegie Hall debut. It was also huge, as it should be."

"Still I feel those self-imposed challenges that are usually in my own head: 'I'm not good enough, I'm not cool enough, I can't, I shouldn't, they won't like me . . . '. Blah blah. The troll in my head rolls out some doozies, but I keep skipping along, thanking God and anyone who'll listen

149

to me thanking them."

"After almost every show, someone will say to me, 'Your music, or song, or book, or show got me through a really hard time, thank you'. That's the BEST feeling because my job is to make people feel stuff. Mostly joy, but a whole range of emotions can flow through someone listening to music. Musicians and songwriters help provide release for people who can't or won't express themselves."

"My creative process, thankfully, is varied and chaotic. I am no good with office hours or prescribed times to write. I write well under pressure, like I have 24 hours to write a keynote speech for a non-profit, or I have 20 minutes to rewrite this show to make it cleaner, but still funny. My muse is a jackass, comes and goes as he pleases, and is always making me write filthy songs full of drunken swearing."

"Music matters to me because . . . it is the hum of my pulse, the heat of my breath and shines a light on everything that matters to me in this world."

Chapter Thirty-Six: Thomas Lauderdale

Credit to Artslandia Magazine and Photo Credit: Amy Graves

Although many expected him to try to become a concert pianist, Thomas Lauderdale never thought of music as a career. Instead, he wanted to become mayor of Portland, Oregon. But the music at the political fundraisers he attended was appallingly lackluster. Enter Pink Martini, a fabulous band infused with fun, multilingual sophistication . . . "a sort of Breakfast at Tiffany's meets the United Nations house band". Since 1994, the band has found a loyal, cult following, and continues to reinvent itself as it enters its 21st year.

"I was adopted in 1970 in Oakland, California. In 1972, we moved to rural Indiana, where my father was a Church of the Brethren minister. My parents were from the earnest side of the 1960s, and had a reel-to-reel player . . . my childhood consisted of Ray Conniff, Ray Charles, Roger Miller, The New Christy Minstrels, The Mormon Tabernacle Choir, and the soundtrack to *Jesus Christ Superstar*, in addition to the hymns of my father's church. So, after church services, I would go up to the piano, trying to pound out the hymns. My parents took this as a sign, and I started piano lessons."

"Even though I loved music and spent most of my childhood practicing, I never thought of music as a real career. When I was in high school in Portland, Oregon, I was very politically-active. I worked in City Hall for Portland Mayor 'Bud' Clark, and I worked for City Commissioner Gretchen Kafoury on the city's first civil rights bill. I served on as many commissions as would have me. I worked on political campaigns. And I wanted to become mayor. I chose not to go to a music conservatory because I felt like the life of a concert pianist was incredibly lonely. I didn't want to be stuck in a practice room with no friends and no parties. So, I went to Harvard where I studied history and literature. Mostly, I threw parties. I graduated in 1992, came back to Portland, and immersed myself in journalism and politics. In 1994, a very conservative organization called the Oregon Citizens Alliance made a nasty attempt to amend the Oregon Constitution and illegalize homosexuality with Measure 13. I had just seen Pee Wee Herman's Christmas Special, which has an unbelievable cavalcade of stars – everybody from Dinah Shore to Whoopi Goldberg to Oprah Winfrey to Little Richard to Magic Johnson to k.d. Lang to Cher and Zsa Zsa Gabor. And the Del Rubio Triplets – three gals, three guitars, somewhere between the ages of seventy and eighty, who wore mini-skirts and little booties and warbled covers of 'Walk Like an Egyptian' and 'Whip It'. I decided to bring them to town to do a series of concerts in retirement homes, hospitals, nursing homes and the occasional Rotary meeting. At the end of each set they would say, 'Please vote no on Measure 13!' It was political activism through entertainment. At the end of the week we had a big, celebratory fundraising concert at a local independent movie house, Cinema 21. I needed an opening act, so I threw on a cocktail dress and Pink Martini was born."

"I thought it was going to be a one-time thing but soon we were asked to play for other political gatherings, benefits for cleaning up the Willamette River, affordable housing, and events for libraries. If there was a political fundraiser for a progressive cause, we probably played it. I mostly thought of it as a fun distraction. After all, I was scampering around in a cocktail dress and we were singing covers of 'I Dream of Jeannie', 'Brazil', and 'Qué Será, Será'. And suddenly we were making money, playing weddings and parties. But it never really occurred to me to travel beyond Portland, Oregon."

"We released our first album in 1997, and suddenly the band was viable. We became popular in France, signed a French record deal, started traveling in Europe, and at a certain point I realized, 'I guess I'm not going to run for office . . . at least not now'. It's amazing – the band has been going for 20 years. Because of the profit-sharing model of the band, I'm very proud to say that everybody in the band has been able to buy a house. And we get to play all around the world, from the Hollywood Bowl to The Cape Cod Melody Tent in Hyannis, Massachusetts, to Oregon farm country, to Paris and Istanbul."

"One of the most wonderful aspects of the band is the opportunity we have had to collaborate with all kinds of amazing people: Jimmy Scott, Jane Powell, Rufus Wainwright, Carol Channing, and Charmian Carr, who played Liesl in *The Sound of Music*, to name a few. Three years ago, I met the von Trapps, the great-grandchildren of Captain and Maria von Trapp. I somehow convinced them to move to Portland, Oregon and we made an album called 'Dream a Little Dream' that we released last year. We also worked with the Oregon Ballet Theatre on a brand-new 45-minute ballet."

"The band's repertoire comes from whatever is going on in our lives. What I'm reading, what I'm looking at . . . all of this inspires and informs the work directly. One day, for example, my friend Patrick Abbey and I were looking through old issues of *Life* magazine and found in a 1964 issue a full-page ad for Hunt's ketchup with the narrative, 'Hang on, little tomato. Stay on the vine until you're fat and juicy. Then we'll pluck you and boil you in secret bubbling spices and turn you into ketchup, and if you're lucky, some smart hamburger may team up with you'. From that, we wrote the song 'Hang On Little Tomato'. Ten years ago, at Everyday Music, my favorite record store, I was in the Japanese section and noticed an album intriguingly titled 'Scat in the Dark' by a woman named Saori Yuki. I couldn't resist. I bought it and fell in love with it. Eventually we covered one of the songs. And when we went to Japan, we met Saori Yuki herself and she asked us to help her produce an album celebrating her 40-

year career. The result was a comeback album that sold half a million copies in Japan."

"One of the strengths of the music is that it's constantly shifting. We sing songs in 25 different languages. The styles change dramatically from song to song, from 'Amado Mio' with all of its splendorous harp and strings, to the 1930s-esque 'Sympathique', an original anthem about not wanting to work, to a piece like 'Hey Eugene', which China wrote, a response to a man named Eugene who never called. Because the repertoire is all over the map stylistically and linguistically, chances are if you don't like one song, you might like the next."

"We named our record label after my dog Heinz. Heinz was a big mutt with a huge head; a golden lab retriever with aspirations of St. Bernard-ism and prehistoric Oregon beaver-ism. Heinz was a great judge of music. If he liked the music, he would lie on his back with his paws towards heaven and his tail would wag. I did several tests with the music before releasing it to make sure he liked it. If he didn't like it, he would become very nervous and pace the borders of the room anxiously. Whenever I went against Heinz, I always paid for it."

"Music matters to me because . . . there's so much bleakness everywhere one turns – I think of Pink Martini as a little beacon of hope. I love the diversity of our audiences – from toddlers, to dogs, to octogenarians and older. Our fans transcend geographic, cultural, and political borders. Our concerts are places where people who normally would never sit next to each other find themselves making friends with people they never imagined themselves befriending."

Chapter Thirty-Seven: David "Lebo" Le Batard

Growing up in South Florida, the son of Cuban immigrants, gave David "Lebo" Le Batard an eclectic mix to draw from on the drafting table that sat in his bedroom. Naturally talented, he loved to illustrate what he saw using cartoons with bold lines of color. Inspired by his culture and its music, the street art, and electric activity that is Miami, his post-modernistic creations reflect this vividness. He gravitates to social performance live art. He has shared the stage with Bela Fleck, The Beastie Boys, Willie Nelson, and Phish while creatively painting to their music. His art can be found in the permanent collections of ESPN, Google, Microsoft, and Sony Music Entertainment. Wherever his art takes him, he conveys his public message of hope and human connection.

"Music is a vital part of my family's history. My grandfather and his four brothers were all in an orchestra called, The Le Batard Orchestra, in Cuba during the 1940s and 1950s. It was a very well-known group; my family's rich musical heritage and our love of music stems directly from my grandfather's orchestra. Music was always playing in our home, which thankfully was a happy one. I remember 1950s rock and roll, as well as older Cuban family music. It was a nice mix."

"Later on, when I was around 13, I can remember buying mix tapes from our neighborhood DJ. Music was pretty neighborhood-specific. In mine it was mostly Miami bass and electronic music. My love of different sounds led to buying mix tapes from DJs in other neighborhoods. I loved how these tapes transported me to other places. They were my first journey away from home. My first stab at independence came from those raunchy lyrics, heavy bass, and the beginning of what was known as ghetto-style music."

"Later in high school I discovered punk rock and hardcore music.

This mix really helped define my philosophy, style of dress, and my 'do it myself' approach to everything that I accomplish. It was this combination of attitude, politics, consciousness, and irreverence, set against a really aggressive musical backdrop, which formed my tastes and perceptions. To this day, I still consider those formative musical experiences as shaping how I look at the world."

"A few years later I discovered be-bop, jazz, and roots reggae. In a way I think these influences had the ethos of punk, but with a much more refined, as well as a spiritual, approach that influenced me. It was these three phases of musical discovery along with a deep interest in studying cartooning that took me into my early 20s. I think, in hindsight, since I wasn't a formally-trained musician, I was looking for a way to take my understanding and love of music and translate it into a visual narrative."

"My greatest teacher has always been my mother. I was raised in a house where we were not only encouraged to discover and follow our interests, but also taught how to home in on those interests and apply discipline to them in a fun and loving way. My mother had a magical way of infusing lessons in smart, creative, and encouraging ways. She always stressed, 'It's not how many times you fall that matters; it's how many times you get up'. It gave me a tremendous sense of empowerment, without the egotistical part that can come with that belief."

"I found my passion for cartooning when I was in fourth grade. I went to a small private school with no real art classes. We had an art cart with some basic art supplies, and a teacher's manual for arts and crafts. That was it. My teacher, Mrs. Hughes, was ornery, chain-smoked cigarettes, and loved to yell. I got into trouble. I was a really hyperactive kid, and drawing was the only thing that calmed me down. For that whole year,

Mrs. Hughes let me sit in the front corner of the classroom, with my desk facing the wall and the art cart blocking me from the rest of the class. She made me the deal that if I finished my work, I could pick out projects to do from the teacher's manual. I loved her so much! This was heaven for me, and I still remember her to this day."

"It was, hands-down, my most memorable year in school. I'd do one of the projects from the book: for instance, I'd make an articulated iguana out of construction paper. One of the kids in the class would say he wanted it. I'd give it to him, and another kid would want one. I'd make another one, but make it a little different than the one I made prior. Eventually I'd made one for every kid in class. Each one was different. I did that with all the projects during the whole year. For me this was the beginning of my path to becoming an artist. It's basically what I continue to do with my art. It's quick and unique."

"I never really had another art class of any impact after fourth grade. I didn't go to school for art. I studied humanities in college, and it definitely taught me how to think like an artist. I also spent time in libraries, learning through books that led the way for me."

"What I've learned and what I try to convey, is that art can be anything. I've painted over 100 guitars. I am always trying to combine art and music. This has led me to doing live painting. I'm all about doing something like improvisational jazz through art. I'm taking classic songs, but infusing them with spontaneity when I perform. It's the artistic discipline coupled with on-the-spot-creativity. It's pure and simple. I follow those cats like Miles, Coltrane, Morgan, Mingus, and Monk. They're where it's at when it comes to my whole approach at live painting."

"For me it's all in the approach. The challenge is to create in the moment. I've painted to a wide variety of music. Of course, the more the music resounds with me, the more I connect with it; but I wouldn't say I have a favorite genre. I like the idea of being able to paint to anything. I can paint to Burning Spear and Willie Nelson. It's really the whole ride that makes me the happiest."

"Music matters to me because . . . it's a universal language that echoes in the soul."

Chapter Thirty-Eight: John Lind

Photo Credit: Manny Keller

John Lind has been playing music for most of his life. But could he have imagined that when he co-founded the Get a Life Marching Band over 20 years ago, that he would play in almost every marching band parade across the country? Could he have believed that the National Association of Music Merchants (NAMM), the world's largest music products trade-only event would ask his band to perform year after year? Could he have dreamed that he would play in the country's most prestigious parade, the 2009 Inaugural parade of Barack Obama? It all happened, and it was possible because of his love of music.

"My dad was a guitar player and he wanted to see if I could get into music somehow, so at first he had me try a lot of different instruments. My dad pushed me to learn the accordion, but it didn't stick. We tried four or five lessons. We tried a trumpet after that, but that didn't stick. Then we tried the drums and I loved it! He saw the opportunity in drumming and paid for my lessons. His generosity allowed me to have five years' worth of professional lessons as a drummer and that helped jump-start my musical career."

"The Get a Life Marching Band got started somewhat by accident. Bob Pulido, my co-director, and I had been members in the One More Time Around Again Marching Band, in Portland, since it first began in 1984. We went to a Drum and Bugle show in Southern California in the early 1990s. Some of the guys in the band were saying that there were not enough gigs for marching bands in this area. You basically got three gigs a year during the Rose Festival Season in the summer and then you're done. Many of my bandmates were thinking, 'Well, hey, we could do more during the summer, and we could get a life'."

"Bob and I put our heads together, and the name Get a Life Marching Band really fit. We thought we could put a band together to play more parades. We talked about getting a grant to help us with buying some drums and equipment. So we asked around, and when Miller Distributing Company gave us $6,000.00, we used that money to get the necessary instruments and started the band in 1994. That was over twenty years ago. We started out with only 13 people!"

"Ever since then, we have participated in just about every major marching band parade in the country from Disneyland, and Walt Disney World, to the Fiesta Flambeau (the largest night parade in the country) and, of course, to Mardi Gras. Even before we started this band I got to march with the One More Time Around Again Marching Band in 1990, in the Tournament of Roses Parade. I can honestly say that I have marched in every major parade in the United States that I have ever wanted to be in."

"I think one of the biggest highlights we have had was that we got an invite to play at the 2009 Presidential Inaugural Parade for Obama. We went to Philadelphia and then we were bussed from Philadelphia to Washington, D.C. I remember it was very, very cold. We weren't dressed for that kind of cold weather. No one told us how cold it could get. I only had a lightweight jacket and I remember it was freezing. But then we started playing. When you get to represent your state, and play songs in front of the President of the United States before those crowds, you don't think about the weather. We were so close to the President's party we could see them wave and smile and they really liked what we did. It was a once-in-a-lifetime experience."

"We have been able to build a great band and I'm proud of what we have accomplished. It shows what two people with an idea and motivation can do. At one point, the biggest the band got to be was around 150-160 people. Right now we have 41 members and of those, 39 of them are performing musicians in their own right. As a marching band, we play a lot of old school and new school tunes. We don't play any Souza marches or anything like that. We play horn-filled soul and funk, and a little R&B on the march. In the last three years, we have not been marching as much. We are doing more stage shows with vocalists who sing those funk and soul tunes. We are playing music from Michael Jackson's 'Thriller' to Stevie Wonder's 'Superstition,' to 'Get Lucky' by Pharrell Williams / Daft Punk and 'Uptown Funk' with Bruno Mars & Mark Ronson."

"Wherever we play we see that it puts a big smile on people's faces. They get what we are talking about through music. They connect with us. They are entertained by the powerful sounds and we hope they walk away feeling like 'Man, I want to hear more of these guys'. That's all we can ask. We think of the audience first in everything we do. We are there to entertain and give them a good time and that fun is contagious. We see music as the connector and we promote it as a lifelong benefit, because that is who we are."

"Music matters to me because . . . I believe that it touches people in a way that nothing else can. Music is a universal language. It moves you. It causes you to dance. It puts a big smile on your face. I believe that music takes you to a new space and time and it makes you feel better about being a human being."

Chapter Thirty- Nine: Riker Lynch

Photo Credit: John Russo

Riker Lynch has been performing for as long as he can remember. Raised in Littleton, Colorado, he and his two younger brothers, Ross and Rocky, and sister, Rydel, would perform in the family's basement charging relatives $1 to see their musical shows. In 2008, when Riker was 16, he begged his parents to go to California so he could pursue his musical passion. The family decided to move together. In 2009, after meeting Ellington Ratliff, or Ratliff, the band R5 found its name. In 2012 they signed with Hollywood Records and have not stopped finding fans. With over four million YouTube views, and one million Instagram followers, their positive feel-good California vibe often brings thousands of fans to see them in venues across the globe including Good Morning America and the American Music Awards.

"I've loved performing since I was three years old. My parents were big Beatles and Elvis fans, so I grew up with great music always playing in the background of my life. My siblings and I would perform any chance we could get. We were all really young, probably four and five when we started putting on our shows together. My parents would invite my relatives over and we all had a blast. When I was 16, we moved to California so we could work on our dream of becoming a band. It seems unbelievable to me that now we are headlining our own world tours in places like Brazil and Argentina."

"I wouldn't say being on stage is for everybody because it is definitely a crazy experience. It is a lot harder than it looks. I love performing so for me being on stage is the coolest thing in the world. Being up there, rocking out with my siblings and best friend, the people I love, in front of a huge crowd of fans, is amazing for me. There is something very special about hearing everybody singing back to me the words that I wrote."

"I love being on tour. It took us about two weeks to prepare for our world tour because we work really well together. We are so familiar with each other we just kind of have that second sense about where it is all going. I construct the show as far as the general layout, what song we are going to open with, and what we will transition to, and how we are going to finish."

"When you're on tour, you are meeting so many different people and you are having so many different experiences, after the show, hanging out in the bus, or talking to kids. All of that becomes part of the creative process for me. I get inspired by other songs I hear, by life experiences, and by people in general. I always try to write a song that makes people feel like they are not the only one going through certain things. At the same time, I also want people to connect with us on an emotional level, as well as enjoy the sound of the song."

"When people listen to the music, I want them to just enjoy it. I am a very optimistic person. I always like to see the glass as half full. I want to make people happy. I think a lot of that comes across in our new song, 'Smile'. So my opening line is, 'Today I feel like running naked through your street just to get your attention'. I want people to feel the adrenaline that I experience when I'm writing the lyrics. I hope people forget the rest of the world for a moment and leave their problems behind for that two- or three-minute song. In our live shows, when I'm playing for about an hour and a half, I have the same goal. We are all invested together in being one positive energy force and connecting with the audience when we perform. It is very inspiring."

"We try to inspire in everything that we do. We teamed up with Office Depot to help kids get inspired and get ready to just rock through the school year. I definitely felt like when I was a kid that I was not that excited about school. We felt that this was important to pump up kids about school."

"Any opportunity we have to connect with people matters to us. I like to chat with people on social media. Every once in a while I just do a random reply on my social media. It is fun. You want people to know that we are here and feeling just like they are. I especially like responding to things that make me laugh, because laughter is one of the greatest things in life. I want the fans to know how much we appreciate them. They are buying tickets. They are coming to the show. They are doing everything to support us and so to just get back and do a tweet I think goes a long way. I don't take that for granted."

"Music matters to me because . . . no matter where you go, everybody loves music. There are tons and tons of different types of music, but everybody loves music."

Chapter Forty: Makana

Photo Credit: Jeff Mallin

At 14, Makana was performing his art of Hawaiian slack key guitar professionally. What began out of musical curiosity at the age of seven became a tireless passion. Makana trained with the masters and honed his craft. He has performed with or opened for some of the greats like Jason Mraz, Jack Johnson, and Sting. He has played at The White House and seen his anthem, "We are the Many", go viral. His music has been featured on three Grammy-nominated albums, including the soundtrack for the Academy Award winning film, "The Descendants", and, in 2012, Makana received Hawaii's top honor, equivalent to a Grammy. His music reflects this cultural and creative diversity.

"I grew up in a very strict household. In terms of music, I was only allowed to listen to religious music or traditional Hawaiian music. I didn't know that any other kind of music existed until I was in high school. Because of that very controlled environment, when I discovered other kinds of music, I got really excited. It really shaped my interest in music. I realized that there was a whole world out there that I had never even considered. I became really, really hungry to learn more about it. Given my focus on Hawaiian music when I was growing up, I was able to build a strong, focused foundation off of traditional Hawaiian music and slack key guitar. That established foundation, combined with the new music I discovered, influenced my creativity. My early structured environment was kind of a blessing in disguise."

"I love the slack key genre because it is also a cultural technique. Like we think of Southern Blues, Slack key guitar originated back in the late 1700s or early 1800s, when the guitar arrived in Hawaii. The Hawaiians got the guitar from the Vaqueros, or Mexican cowboys. The cowboys had their own style of playing. They had open tunings. The Hawaiians adapted those tuning techniques and created new ones that had their own feeling, their own vibe. They taught themselves how to play bass, rhythm, and melody at the same time on a single guitar. When you hear slack key guitar, typically it is played on a single guitar and there are three parts going on, so it is almost like simulating three guitars in one. It has a really full sound."

"Slack key is difficult to do because it takes many years to actually train your hand to be able to play all the three parts at once, and there are very few teachers. In fact, maybe 50 years ago, if you looked back to the liner notes of some of the records that were out, they called it 'a dying art form' back then, and that is when more of the masters were still alive. So there are very few players. This is a very personal music, and many of the old time masters did not want to share their own personal techniques. They were very private about it. I was very blessed to be able to learn from some of the masters."

"My brand of music, Slack Rock, is kind of a buzz term for the way that you approach the guitar. I used the techniques that I learned in slack key and expanded them. When I am not playing traditional music, and just doing my own thing or interpreting other people's forms, it is more of a kind of high-energy style. I create sound to build the illusion that there are two, three or four people on stage, without using any loopers or digital trickery. I always had this dream of being able to have a huge sound alone. Using what I learned from the traditional slack key, I fused it with other genres and styles like blues, rock and bluegrass to create my own sound."

"Once I create a song and put it out there, I let it go. Then whatever people get out of it, they get out of it. Certainly it is none of my business what they get out of it. You know what I mean? You just can't control that. It's not in your power. You put every ounce of your soul and energy

171

into the music and then after that you let it go. The best thing you can hope for is that it resonates with people and inspires them, and then whatever they get out of it is totally personal. I love that everybody gets something different from it. That's my favorite part about music."

"Music inspires people. It can convey a powerful message with emotion and motivate people to act. Emotion is mostly what controls the human world, and music is a powerful conveyer of human emotion. I use my music for community outreach. Many of my performances are to support causes for the environment. I do work for the reefs in Hawaii. I am a dedicated food activist, and advocate for social justice and music education. I like using my music for something greater than myself, to bring inspiration to others, and help good causes."

"My philosophy has always been to build direct relationships with your fans. Don't let anybody get between that. Take care of your friends well, be generous, and focus on your craft. I have been performing and creating music for 29 years now. A lot of people think that after singing for a few months, they are ready to do a record or something. I feel it is important to have a strong foundation; to not just be able to sing or play a guitar or a piano, but to be able to bring your own spirit and personality into your music. People want a piece of you, and you have to communicate that through your music. It is more than just going up on a stage and playing or singing a song. There is the inspirational, emotional element which is really important and that is what people need and want to connect with."

"Music matters to me because . . . it is like breathing for me. I need to do it to be alive. I am more in harmony with myself creating music than I am doing anything else in this world. It's who I am."

Chapter Forty-One: David K. Mathews

As a very young child David K. Mathews found all kinds of music appealing; blues, pop, jazz, rock and roll: it all mattered to him. He never went to music school. In fact, he left high school early and pursued his dream. Little did he know that he would be tapped to join one of the world's most renowned artists, Carlos Santana, as the lead keyboardist of the Santana Band.

"I have been playing music since I was seven, and I'm now 55 years old! Neither one of my parents is particularly musical, so I didn't start taking lessons until I was about eight. However, I did listen to a lot of music in the early 1960s. My dad liked Scottish bagpipe music and John Philip Sousa marches. I also remember my dad playing the records of Jelly Roll Morton, and Louis Armstrong. My folks always had the radio on during the daytime. I can distinctly remember hearing all of that rock, soul, and R & B on AM radio as I was growing up. They had a much more varied playlist in those days. I would listen to people like Frank Sinatra, Nat King Cole, Perry Como, and that's how I actually learned to play those great songs. At that time, I didn't understand what an important part of our American cultural fabric this music is, but I sure got exposed to a variety of genres: Bach, Led Zeppelin, Al Green, Jimi Hendrix, and James Brown."

"All of that music really influenced me. Melody was always floating around in my head. I just knew at an early age that I probably wanted to play music for the rest of my life. I stopped lessons after I turned 13, since I was pretty much playing by ear, and by the time I was about 17, I was playing gigs professionally in Top 40 bands. I dropped out of high school. I was thrown out actually, so I only have a 10th grade education. I was in high school for two years, but I just started playing and trying to make a living playing music and I have been working on it ever since. I love all

kinds of music: classical, jazz, pop, Afro-Cuban, gospel, blues, R & B. I
like everything."

"I got a job playing with the band Tower of Power in the early 1980s.
I was 23. In 1988 I joined with Etta James. We played for 19 years
together. I think our last gig was probably in 2009 when she had to retire.
My name was floating around when Carlos was looking to add to the
band. I grew up listening to Santana on the radio and I was always playing
his music. I had friends who were in the band. I had always expressed an
interest in playing with the group. The keyboard player I had replaced in
1983 in Tower of Power had actually left to join Santana in 1983, and he
ended up leaving Santana in 2009. There were about six guys out of 11
guys in the band that I had played with in various bands based in the San
Francisco area, all of whom I have known anywhere from 15 to 20 years. I
told these friends how much I wanted to join them in the band."

"Even though I expressed an interest in playing with the band, I never
expected that I would get a call. But then one day one of the guys told me
to expect a call from the management. When it happened I couldn't
believe it. I remember our conversation. He said, 'You come highly
recommended, and we would like you to start playing with the band in
about three or four weeks. We'll send you a bunch of CDs so you can
listen to the music we're doing now. Just learn the music and be ready to
play'. That was it. I never auditioned."

"For my first gig I had no rehearsals. I met with Carlos and a couple
of other guys briefly beforehand, and worked on a couple of tunes. They
sort of checked me out. Then I went on the road to Las Vegas and played
with them for a couple of weeks. That was my breaking-in period. In my
spare time, I was busy writing out charts to all of the Santana songs so that

I would be prepared. When I did my first gig, I was pretty much reading everything. I had written and transcribed material from records they had sent me. But it was just a good fit right away. I have been there for four years now."

"I have to say that being in Carlos's band and with the organization is kind of like, in terms of a career move, being a baseball player. You know you have been playing with some really great teams in AA and AAA ball, and with some really renowned players, when suddenly you get that call to go up to join the Boston Red Sox during their World Series season. You just need to be prepared and be ready to do it. I always felt that if you're ready with your instrument and learn how to play as well as you can, your work will speak for itself. Eventually and hopefully you get that lucky break and get that call to the Big League. That's what happened to me. I am very happy about it. I am very grateful. It has been a high point in my career and certainly a great opportunity for me."

"Carlos is consumed by music. He listens to music more than anybody I know. He is constantly listening to music before the gig, and after the gig. He has his iPod and he listens voraciously to a variety of music. Certainly we love many of the same things: Miles Davis, John Coltrane, Bob Marley, and Jimi Hendrix. He loves BB King, Wayne Shorter, and he also loves all types of Afro-Cuban music. On the one hand, he loves the Temptations. On the other hand, he loves world music. I think he puts all these influences into his playing. He has very broad interests and is a pretty driven guy."

"When it comes to putting his music out there, he has ideas about how he wants the music to sound, and there is a spiritual component in there too. When he plays, he reminds me of Dexter Gordon, in the sense that he quotes musical phrases from other songs. He is a melody-maker. He plays more like a singer than a guitar player. He is constantly trying to push the limits of note combinations. He's always thinking in terms of a dominant melody, and he comes up with new ideas all the time through experiments. He has a singing tone and likes to play the long sustained notes. It's inspiring. I have learned about musical projection, and how to take a simple idea and express it in broad strokes of primary sounds so that people can understand it. He is constantly trying to do something that's satisfying to him."

"We don't normally do a lot of rehearsing. Occasionally we will have a day or so rehearsal before we go out on a tour, but we have a really large repertoire, pretty much all of the hit songs that he has had over the years. He hits on the highlights and known tunes since the 1960s. But that is all part of our active repertoire. If we were to rehearse, it wouldn't be possible, because there is so much. We might get an email from Carlos, asking us to learn this tune so we can try it this afternoon, but most of our rehearsal is done while we are traveling. That keeps it interesting."

"Music matters to me because . . . it's my life."

Chapter Forty-Two: Bibi McGill

Bibi McGill is an internationally-known musician who, as musical director and lead guitarist in Beyoncé's all-female band, also finds time to work as a wellness educator, tirelessly promoting yoga as an acclaimed yoga teacher. Bibi's creativity also inspired her to start her own health food company. Music provides her with a lifeline that combined with yoga and a healthy lifestyle keeps her grounded. She believes everyone should live a balanced life no matter the circumstance. Bibi is an active leader in Street Yoga, a nonprofit that makes yoga available to at-risk youth.

"I don't really remember a time when I was growing up where there wasn't music in my house. My older brother and sister played classical piano. My grandfather played many instruments. We always had lots of vinyl playing in the house. I was lucky to be able to see live music at a young age, too. I have been playing the guitar since I was 12 years old. I went to school and graduated from the University of Colorado, and then moved to Los Angeles to try to make things happen. In 2001, I landed my first big break with Pink, and after that my career really began."

"I had been involved with female artists like Pink before I went into Latin music. I worked with La Ley for about three years. After that, I became the musical director and lead guitarist of Beyoncé's all-female band. Prior to Beyoncé, I had taken a break from touring and playing because the lifestyle difference was really getting to me. I had found yoga in 1998. I took my first yoga class and was hooked. I then became a certified teacher and began to focus on that part of my life."

"In 2006, I got a call that Beyoncé was putting together an all-female band, but my first thought was, 'Not a chance'. I liked Beyoncé and her music, but I was not interested in playing the guitar or touring again. But my dad really wanted me to try, and so I decided to go to the audition. I remember that she had one audition in Los Angeles, and when I got there I realized I was supposed to be there. I played my best and got selected from over 1200 women. I've been with her for eight years."

"Everyone in the music industry is different, so each job is always a unique experience. I am constantly on the road. I don't consider myself a star. It feels like I've been working very hard for many years to get to do something I really enjoy. But it's difficult work. Generally we rehearse for three to six weeks, every day, all day, before a tour. We go over everything and rehearse the entire show. We have to keep up with Beyoncé's fast-paced schedule, so the first thing you learn is to stay focused. I love it. It's been a fun learning experience and I've grown as a musician. Traveling to different places and seeing different people and cultures really teaches you things about yourself. I've come to realize that people have lots of similarities."

"Since I'm so busy, I am very aware of what I do. I make sure that I monitor what I put in my body, what I do with my body, as well as who and what I surround myself with. I make sure that I don't do anything to drain my energy, so I can channel it into the places it is needed. Yoga gives me that creative outlet to channel these different energies. It provides the balance that I need in my life. I'm so busy I make sure to save time for doing the things I really enjoy, too!"

"I'm inspired by things that are natural, healthy, and make people feel good. I am a total health-nut. A few years ago, I started my own food processing business for health-food snacks called BiBi Kale Chips: a raw, vegan, gluten-free, organic snack. It came about by accident. I had a bunch of extra kale in my garden that I didn't want to go to waste, so I researched how to make my own chips with the ingredients I liked. The first batch came out great. The word began to spread, and in five weeks they were on the shelves in Portland stores."

"Music matters to me because . . . it is a creative way for me to express myself, as well as a way to connect with others. It is a language that is not only seen and felt, but is also unseen and felt. It gives us the power to change for the better."

Chapter Forty-Three: Dave Metzger

Dave Metzger found his passion at 12. It began with choir at his Corvallis, Oregon middle school. His teacher, Joyce, inspired his musical imagination. A gifted writer, who could weave together dramatic sounds, Dave immersed himself in learning every genre. Dave was 16 when the movie *Star Wars* came out. The sweeping cinematic scores captivated him. As the credits rolled, he knew he had found his career. He has become one of Hollywood's top arrangers and worked on 60 films. Dave's music can be found in many legendary movies, most recently, the critically-acclaimed and award-winning *Frozen*.

"I really tried to learn as much as I could about different styles of music, so that when the opportunities presented themselves, I was ready. At 31, I got my big break. I was called to write for *The Tonight Show* with Jay Leno. After about five years of working on the show and creating around 250 arrangements, another door opened. I worked on the Broadway version of *The Lion King*. I orchestrated that production when I was 37 years old and was nominated for a Tony Award for Best Orchestration."

"I love my job because every day is different. I get to work for a variety of companies such as Disney, Dreamworks, Warner Brothers, Sony, and 20th Century Fox. More importantly, I love my job because every project is different. I wear many different hats. On some movies, I am just an orchestrator. What that means is that I take the sketch that is already written by the composer, and therefore most of the creative work with writing the lines is done. I write the final score, which takes anywhere between two and three weeks typically. For other movies, I compose additional music when the composer does not have time to do all of the composition. A typical time-frame on a movie like that might be between three and six months. On a movie like *Frozen*, though, where I was much more creatively involved, I worked 14-hour days for over six months on that project. I did the arranging and orchestrating."

"Getting started is always the hardest part for me. Think of a painter who is looking at a blank canvas, wondering where to start. It is very similar to composing music. A typical movie is going to have 60-80 minutes of music in it, so there's pressure to write that much music in a short period of time. Writing music for films is all very deadline-specific, due to movie release dates. My inspiration comes from knowing I have to get it done, and that the deadline is immovable."

"I was brought into the project by Tom MacDougall, who is a music executive at Disney Feature Animation. I hadn't met Bobby Lopez and Kristen Anderson-Lopez before starting work on *Frozen*. All I got from them was an audio file of a piano part and a vocal sketch. My job at that point was to take those piano parts and then arrange them for a full orchestra. In movie scores, you typically have 80-90 musicians playing. Having had experience working in both worlds, I knew how to turn a Broadway sound into something cinematic."

"The best part for me is going to the recording session. The cool thing about the recording session is that it is the pinnacle of all the time that you've been working alone. When you are surrounded by a full orchestra, you finally get to hear what you have been working on. The musicians bring a stunning musicality to the project. They really are the ones who bring the whole thing to life. They're so talented. There is no practicing beforehand. They just show up in the recording session, sit down, look at the music, and just start playing it. The score was 500 pages. That is definitely the most exciting and rewarding part of the whole process for me."

"Music matters to me because . . . I could not imagine what life would be without it."

Chapter Forty-Four: Mikronesia

Photo Credit: Megan Cauley

When the electroacoustic musician, Michael McDermott, known by his stage name, Mikronesia, received a call from Mike Ferrare, and his advertising company, Agency Magma, he did not know what to expect. This was not a music label. Magma wanted to find a way to deliver a positive mindset to the consumer of the ALO beverage. It had to be authentic and sincere. They were the architects of an intriguing campaign and found the answer lay in sound. They hired Mikronesia, believing he would be the perfect artist to create original music for each ALO product. Known as ALOtones, these drink-specific musical songs express the refreshing aspect of the beverage in a thoughtful, musical harmony. Mikronesia has created a musical feeling for every flavor.

"My path into music began early. I think I knew that was what I always wanted to do. My dad was a drummer, so I was exposed to a variety of music growing up. I took piano, bass, and drum lessons. I favored the soundtracks of those suburban rock bands that were popular when I was growing up. I played in bands through high school and college at Philadelphia University and Berklee College of Music. I learned about music theory and composition, and was exposed to many different teachers depending on my instrument. I was always performing, learning, writing, and playing music. It was continuously changing but it was always what I wanted to do."

"This project was exciting because it was so different. Normally when creating sound, like film scoring, or making music for dance, I'm looking at something and responding to what's happening visually. In this case, I only had the drink and the marketing copy on the bottles. I didn't have any visuals. I drank ALO to help me come up with a sound to reflect this product. I knew it was more of a sipping drink that you chill with. It's something you take slower. You don't slam it. That was my inspiration point."

"One thing I noticed was that the drink had texture. That became a creation starting point for me. I focused on the texture and thought about how someone would feel when tasting the drink. I wanted the music to express shifting layers of sound, in addition to the varied beats. We all know that the number one thing to transform a mood or a moment is music. Music is most powerful."

"I thought, 'what if it became a part of the drink? Will it work? Is it worthy of being a piece of art?' We didn't want to make it feel like an ad. I'm not a commercial music guy. I knew they weren't looking for a jingle in the same way as for advertising bubble gum or Coca-Cola. At the end of the day it was a sincere concept. It's not a promotion where you pop a top and get Britney Spears's new hit single. Music is authentically part of the drink."

"I started with figuring out the notes of flavor in ALO Exposed, their flagship flavor. It is very pure, just ALO and honey. Another drink, Optimistic Bloom, has pomegranate and cranberries. It has a brighter, sweeter taste to it. I used the brightness of sounds to add dimension to the drink. I wanted to deliver a positive mindset. Making music a part of the drink makes it worthy of being a piece of art. I hope people share the music and connect with it, and with each other. It is art, first and foremost."

"This creative process was a great challenge for me. The music industry has changed drastically. I have a record label called Earsnake. The traditional model where you go to the record store and buy an album as a personal keepsake on your shelf, or lend it to a friend, is non-existent. Everything is online. It's what people do. We share music. Everyone expects to stream music. It has become really difficult to get your music out there as an artist. It was exciting to create the unique sounds and produce the drink-specific songs for ALO. This wasn't like, 'we want your song and we'll slap it on the label as a gimmick'. This was creating something specifically to express the product's uniqueness through sound."

"Music matters to me because . . . it always brings connection."

Chapter Forty-Five: June Millington

Photo Credit: Marita Madeloni
190

It's almost as if June Millington and music are fused and one can't be thought of without the other. Born in Manila the eldest of seven, June began performing on the ukulele with her sister, Jean, at family gatherings. When she heard the sound of the guitar, she had an epiphany, and knew it would be her salvation. She got her first one when she was 13, and, from that point on, it never left her side. In 1969, she co-founded and played as lead guitarist of the all-female rock band, Fanny, one of the first to be signed by a major label and the first to record an entire album. She has provided a foundation for future generations of female rockers, co-founding the Institute for Musical Arts, a nonprofit foundation that supports women and girls in music.

"I always loved music from a very young age. My sister Jean and I discovered we could play songs off the radio on our ukuleles. We got a kick out of singing and playing hits of the day, especially to our family. It was our secret joy. I remember in 6th grade hearing a sound that called out to me. It actually got me out of my chair and I began walking towards it – I didn't even ask permission to get up, which was a no-no at this very strict school in Manila. I was attending Assumption Convent, the one year that we went to a Catholic girls' school, which many members of my mother's family had attended. Surprisingly, no one said anything to me; it was as if I was invisible in that moment. I followed that sound down the hall and was astonished to see a girl playing by herself in an empty room. I stood there listening, absolutely riveted, and thought this, exactly: 'Why didn't anyone tell me?'"

"After that experience, I knew playing guitar was my calling. The only requirement for inspiration is to be ready to receive it. I don't find it – it finds me. If I sit still long enough, I hear it in the silence. Inspiration is everywhere, if you would but listen and receive. This is how it began for me. So many things just happen on the path you follow if you are open to them."

"When we formed The Svelts in 1964, my sister and I both wanted to play guitar. I had moved from acoustic to electric guitar and Jean to bass. We simply flipped a coin, and I won. If I hadn't, that would've changed everything. Jean is simply one of the best bass players ever, so we're lucky everything happened the way it did."

"Being a pioneer is rough. You have to be tough like a diamond, to be on-point. You get all the potshots. There was a tremendous amount of prejudice during those times. Being a Filipino-American rocker just wasn't that common. Conversely, it's really fun when the energy gets converted on the spot. It's the same energy transformed at least 10 times – you can feed on it, and use it as a sling, so to speak. But it's also a bit lonely. No matter what, it's up to you – you have to do the work, keep exploring, and pushing the envelope. First you find the envelope, then push! That's why it's good to be in a band, because it gives you company. However, you'd better be like-minded, or the band won't last."

"I didn't start out to be an inspiration. Initially, music was our lifeline to our classmates and then to the world. It just made us feel so good. Once I really started to write, I'd think about conveying a particular feeling that was arising. I had many musical influences around me to draw from, like 'Tom Dooley', 'Follow the Drinking Gourd', 'Stewball', 'Puff the Magic Dragon', by Peter, Paul, and Mary, all the early Belafonte hits, and early pop rock, like 'Travelin' Man', by Rickie Nelson."

"Music is just a magical form of communication. So whether I write and sing about love, world peace, ending violence, pride in being a brown woman ('Brown Like Me'), ending oppression, building unity ('Building on a Rainbow Bridge'), or talking about being a girl who can rock and be free to express herself ('Play Like a Girl'), it's just a perfect vehicle of expression. I would hope all who listen would feel happiness and feel better about themselves. From that perspective, I want to do something good and positive."

"IMA, of which I'm a co-founder (1987), came out of that feeling. It 'exists for all women in music and music-related business'. From that seed we've created something that responds to the needs of women. It's pretty vast, and complicated, but it's working. We create a safe space, keep cleaning up our own inner space, and put all the skills we have to work. That may sound simple, but indeed it's not – if it were, more people would do it! One of the keys is trust: in ourselves, and in the outcome. Honest communication is essential. So is laughter."

"There is really only one story to tell, over and over: 'There's hope if we try, if we do it together'; 'do good, don't hurt others, treat everyone well'. Do not budge from that position. That's the story, told in myriad ways. It's the only one that lasts. Everything else causes self-destruction."

"So, we must create, and that only comes out of light. And that light is us! There's where we pick up the responsibility. We, as narrators, as those who have chosen to be expanders of consciousness, have come quite far. I'm not sure how far the audience has come though. I believe that we can play like a girl and change the world. That is a motto for me."

"Without the gift of the fluidity in music, which is so generous and nonjudgmental, everything would be in pieces. That includes me. I use music for everything: to walk down the stairs, to remember things, to get my mind and body in motion and in sync. We need music to hold everything together, even on a cellular level. Its miracle, seemingly so invisible, is what allows us to become miracles and interact with one another. The more you know about it, the more you can vibrate on a higher and more efficient plane. Music really is the key to everything."

"Music matters to me because . . . it leads me directly to life, to all things living, to dreams, and to what is possible."

Chapter Forty-Six: Mike Mitchell

The song 'Louie Louie' is the most-recorded song in rock history. There is even a Louie Louie Report for all things Louie-related. The song has history and mystery. There is subterfuge with unintelligible lyrics, the FBI controversy, and the song being banned from play in many states in the early 1960s. Mike Mitchell, of the Kingsmen, is a part of all of that intrigue. As an original member of the Kingsmen, he has played with The Rolling Stones, The Beach Boys, The Four Seasons, and many other bands that mark genres of music. The Kingsmen's recording of 'Louie Louie' is one of the most famous – and it happened almost by accident.

"Music was pretty much everything for me. I was one of those kids who took up guitar when I was about 10 years old and started playing it all the time. There just wasn't much going on when I was in school. I started with country music because the teachers really only taught orchestra music. A few friends and I put the band together in 1959, when we were in high school. It emerged very simply. It came from some high school friends who just wanted to play music around school together. Lynn was the drummer and I had played guitar. Lynn had another friend who played guitar, and he talked a friend into playing bass. Eventually we had a piano player join us. That was it."

"'Louie Louie' didn't start out as the famous cult song that it is today. Like most things, it was just one thing after another that happened along the way. We started out like any band does, playing local gigs. As we got better, we began working as the house band in a teen nightclub, The Chase. We played five nights a week. It was owned by a KISN local radio station disc jockey, Ken Chase. Chase, whose real name was Michael Korgan, was personally responsible for us recording 'Louie'. He also produced the record, including coming into the studio to raise the microphone above Jack's head so that the lyrics were unintelligible.

Another KISN disc jockey, Roger Hart, managed the band Paul Revere and the Raiders, and thought it was a good idea and took their band into the same studio to record the song two days later."

"'Louie Louie' was a pretty popular song in the Northwest. There were half a dozen artists who had recorded it before us. We liked it, and learned it by listening to The Wailers' rendition on a jukebox. The Wailers were a big production band from Tacoma, Washington. They were our go-to guys. We really looked up to them. After we learned 'Louie Louie' from the jukebox, we perfected it and then went down to a studio to put something together. We needed to make a demo tape for a job on a cruise ship. In 35 minutes we cut four songs. The whole session cost us $36.00."

"After we made the tape, Chase (Korgan) took it right to the KISN radio station and started playing it. It was met with some local applause and eventually it made its way to a guy who owned a record company out in Seattle, Washington. He loved it and put it on his label. It then got shipped to Wand, a record label in New York. Somehow it ended up being played in Boston. The station was running the worst records of the day list, and so our version of 'Louie Louie' came up. Well, when it played that first time, it lit up all of the phone lines. The Boston radio station called the New York label and asked if they had 'Louie Louie' and they said, 'Yes, it's here in the garbage'. They actually had thrown it in the garbage can because they thought it was so bad that it wouldn't become much of anything. They had to pull it out!"

"The song ended up getting great reviews, and the stations started playing it all the time. We were selling records in Boston like crazy and it just gradually worked its way across the county. I was 19 at the time, and we immediately went out on the road and started working. It didn't stop

197

for five years. We were called a garage band at the time, because of the way the song sounded. 'Louie Louie' proved that you could go into your garage with a tape-recorder, make music, and record it. That was it."

"The song inspired kids. Rock and Roll was very much influenced by kids. It's kids who made it happen. And that is what we did. Also, because the song only used three chords, it was easy to play. It became the theme song for marching bands and really for the high school experience. It was a beginning song for guys who wanted to play bass, guitar, or drums, because it was so simple. Music is lifeblood. It's worldwide. It's for everybody. Everybody can feel one kind of music or another and relate to it."

"We went through a time that we liken to Beatlemania. There was a lot of craziness going on. We couldn't walk down the street. It was pretty intense. It was really fun, too. There was always a group of people screaming and hollering for us. We played six nights per week. This meant we had to travel about 500 miles per day by bus. We'd get to a city and check into a Holiday Inn, go to sleep for a little bit, wake up, do a sound check, then play a show. We'd do the same thing over and over again. We played 40 weeks out of the year."

"Music matters to me because . . . it's my life. We've been together as a band for 50 years. I don't know what else I would have done had it not been for music."

Chapter Forty-Seven: Sean Moeller

Rock Island, Illinois does not immediately conjure up images of cutting-edge music. Yet, Sean Moeller's Daytrotter has made Rock Island the place to be if you are a musician. With a passion for all music genres and a talent for finding innovative sounds, Sean's idea to use minimalist recording for live sessions has been called a "real-time snap- shot of modern music." The website has won many honors and awards, but Sean's approach remains the same as when he began: stay true to the music.

"My musical environment growing up was limited mainly to listening to the radio. My dad had a small record collection that he kept from his college years. But really, as a child growing up, music was one of those things that I just didn't feel at the time. I did a 180-degree change in middle school because, after that, it was always about music for me. In high school, The Blue Album came out, and that cemented everything for me. When I went off to college, I finally had great record stores that I could just go to whenever I wanted. Then it just got out of control. I became a huge music fan. Some of my favorite rap groups were Das Efx and The Pharcyde. I started to be a big Doors fan, so I had the double CD by the Doors. If you ask anyone today what his or her favorite music is, it will be so different then what mine was at the same age because of the Internet. I think the answer would be 'My gosh, all I do is listen to music!' I just go from one record to another. For me during that time, finding music was about relying so much more heavily on people to introduce you to new things. A lot of that is what I'm trying to do with Daytrotter; to be that person who introduces you to something new."

"I launched Daytrotter in 2006. When I'm asked what my inspiration for starting Daytrotter was, I have to admit it was born out of a little bit of boredom. I was just out of college and spending my time writing for a local newspaper. I thought that was what I was going to do be doing, just writing for a newspaper, and a bunch of alternative weeklies. During that time everybody was sounding the death knell of newspapers and print media. It made me stop and think. I looked around and realized that I couldn't have a family and really survive on what I made at the newspaper. It was not an intention to try and make more money – that was certainly not the case. It was more like to try and build something and do something that I really loved. I hoped that maybe it would turn into something a little bit bigger. The pure inspiration was to write about bands that I thought were great."

"I was getting frustrated at the newspaper because I was trying to pitch new bands. I wanted to be different. There were already lots of stories written about bands that everybody knew. Nine years ago, online journalism was not nearly as prevalent as it is now. Today there are links for everyone, and everybody is writing about everybody. It has gone in completely the opposite direction. You could barely exist and everybody is writing about you. That is not the way it was nine years ago. I think this is hampering bands in a different way, and that makes Daytrotter even more relevant. Our concept at Daytrotter remains the same; every band is still handpicked. We are a website that has lots of recordings to choose from and we make the bands available for everyone to listen to. Daytrotter is my vision of an online magazine: the source for new music discovery from the best emerging bands. We have 4400 sessions posted. Every band has been invited to come to us for a live session before they are put on the website. I am still discovering new music. It's what I do."

"I get inspired every day by every band that comes in. At this point, we are into so many bands, that when I hear it has become a musical goal for bands to come into a session, I feel very rewarded. Everyday somebody comes in that you have a really great conversation with, you give a little bit of yourself, and they are sharing their music. I don't think most people get that in their daily lives. I think most people get in their car, get on a train, get to work, clock in, do their shift and leave. Maybe if you're lucky, you have something that sort of inspires you. Every day for me is inspiring because of music. I meet so many really great people. I've made friendships with people that I never thought I would meet."

"Music matters to me because . . . it is really the core of existence. No matter what kind of person you are, I think everybody wants to be understood. I think if everyone could just be understood, there would be fewer problems. Music is an amazing form of expression and it is hard not to love that."

Chapter Forty-Eight: Ray Nelson

Ray Nelson loves music. What began with a guitar lesson would lead to a 30-year career in the industry, and then founding an international nonprofit called Guitars Not Guns. Ray finds unique ways to make music come alive. He wrote an album called "Sing out for Motorcycles", and the artist's conception on the album's cover inspired him to go one step further and turn a motorcycle into a guitar that could be ridden. With some help from friends, Ray spent over one year building his "guitar bike". He rode it from San Francisco to New York City landing him in Ripley's Believe it or Not and on the Discovery Channel plus several magazine and newspaper articles. Not satisfied with that accomplishment, he decided to transform a 1968 Ford into another drivable vehicle: the guitar car. The mayor of Palm Beach County, City of Lake Worth, Florida, designated October 21 as Guitars Not Guns Day. Ray delivers the gift of music to people in any way he can.

"My parents were musically-inclined. When I was seven, they showed me a few chords on the guitar, and since that time I've always had it as a part of my life. I spent 30 years in the music business. I started playing professionally as the Ray Nelson Combo in St. Louis. I've worked as a recording artist, as an actor, as a TV host; all of the jobs that go with making a living as an entertainer. In 2004, I built a guitar-car out of a 1968 Ford. In 1981, I built a motorcycle guitar. In 1982, I rode the motorcycle guitar in from San Francisco to New York and back. It's ten feet long. It's in *Ripley's Believe It or Not* as the only guitar ridden from coast to coast. I can certainly say that music has been my big part of my life."

"What inspired me to create the Guitars Not Guns project, was that my wife and I became foster parents after I retired from playing music. In a matter of six months, we had four teenagers who were long-term foster kids, in our home. They all arrived with one thing in common: they just had a few clothes in a plastic bag, and that was it. I couldn't believe it. Of course, being in the industry and being around music all my life, I knew the power of music, so I went out looking for guitars to give to them. When I saw the look on their faces and I saw how music allowed them to express themselves, I knew I had to do more. It changed their lives and mine. I decided that I wanted to give the opportunity of music to any foster kid who wanted one."

"We started in 2000 in San Jose, California. I had a bunch of donated guitars and a small room in the city's social services building. The next class started in Santa Cruz. This has been a grassroots movement. It started growing on its own, as people wanted to get involved with helping kids. We spread from county to county and now have over 30 chapters in 15 different states in the U.S. We also have chapters in Canada. We're still growing."

"Guitars Not Guns turns around the lives of a lot of kids. We know that music has the power to heal, and our program does that. Music is an alternative to violence. The kids we deal with are underprivileged, at-risk youth – usually foster kids – who don't have many opportunities. We provide them with something to keep them busy. It is a proven fact that if you learn to play an instrument, you do better in school. My motto is, 'We may not put clothes on their back or food in their stomachs, but what we do give them is good for the soul and lasts a lifetime'."

"Guitars Not Guns provides every child that signs up for the beginning eight-week program with a new guitar. No one is turned away. The child can keep the guitar at the end of the session, if they have learned the six chords and a of couple songs that we require of them. We have a graduation ceremony before they go to level two. We give them a big celebration and a certificate to empower them. If they've learned the chords and performed the two songs, they get to keep the guitar forever. It's not like we give them the guitar. They earn the guitar. If they don't earn it, they have to turn it back in."

"Music matters to me because . . . when words don't work, music does."

Chapter Forty-Nine: Tim Nordwind

Tim Nordwind found music's benefits early. He attended an art camp at age 11 and immersed himself in songs. There he met his future bandmate, Damian Kulash. The story goes that the boys stayed connected through the years and, in 1998, formed their band, OK Go, in Chicago. The band's name reflects the love of art originating from a camp art teacher, who would encourage the students with the words "Ok, go!" This creative joy fostered at a young age would grow and expand artistic boundaries. Their viral videos break the mold by incorporating art and music in single-shot takes that are awe-inspiring. OK Go won a 2007 Grammy Best Music video, and a 2014 MTV VMA for best video visual effects for "The Writing's On the Wall" video.

"Music is something that is therapeutic in my life. When I was growing up I went through some difficult experiences in my family. My mother passed away when I was 12. Music was generally a place I would turn to for comfort and solace. Eventually I began writing music as my therapy, and that is around the time when I got really involved with learning how to play guitar and writing music. I don't know if I looked at it as a form of therapy at the time, but when I think about it now I realize that music definitely provided therapy. It gave me a way of expressing emotion and being in the moment, whether it was a moment of levity or a moment of sadness. If I didn't feel like writing music, then I would listen to music. It was always about music. It helped me process my feelings."

"What I really love about music and find intoxicating is that it's so immediate. Within a matter of seconds you can communicate so many different types of emotion. I love the catharsis of sharing a feeling."

"As a band, we try to express that emotional aspect of music through our songs and videos. I don't think it's necessary to have history together, but I feel it can play a very important role. I think in our case it does play an absolutely monumental role in why we've been a band for over 16 years. I've known Damian since I was 11. Our relationship is very special. We have known each other for 27 years. He knows my family, including my mother before she passed away, and I know his, and we act like family together. It means that like most families, we love each other, but also sometimes get into disagreements or debates. But we're always able to work through our differences together. I trust him enough that if he is fighting for a creative idea, even if I don't understand it right at the moment, it is worth following because we have that history of enjoying each other's creative work. I think he sees the same qualities in me. It makes us good creative partners."

"OK Go is four guys who share similar interests. What gets us out of bed in the morning is the fact that we enjoy the creative process and making stuff. We love chasing our most exciting ideas. Sometimes the ideas get pretty crazy. For our video 'The Writing's On the Wall', it took three weeks to build a set of optical illusions using every day household objects. We had nine costume changes and over 50 people to help us with this project. We shot it as a one take music video but it took about 60 takes to get it right. It's a lot of work, but the entire process is really fun for us."

"I hope the take away from our music and videos is a sense of joy and wonderment. There are definitely different ways that music can help. For people who are feeling happy, I hope our music can help them continue to feel happy. For people who are feeling sad, I hope it can help them to understand they are not alone in their sadness, there is hope, and that will make them feel comforted. Everybody comes to a song with his or her own history and experiences. I hope our songs are universal enough so that someone can listen to it and feel, 'Yeah, yeah, me, too'."

"Music matters to me because . . . it has been there for me through both good times and bad; moments of celebration, sadness, reflection, love. Music is so healthy. It's helped me to feel in so many ways and live a fuller and more fulfilling life."

Chapter Fifty: Michael Orland

Photo Credit: Ray Garcia

Michael Orland's story begins with the film, *Mary Poppins*. He first saw it as a four-year-old, with his mother. He was mesmerized. He went the next day with his grandmother. He went the next week with his father. He went back with his grandmother again and again. His house became filled with the movie's soundtrack. He played every song on the piano, by ear. His parents encouraged his musical gift and he followed his heart, leaving college early to pursue his dream. Like the *Idol* kids he mentors, he believed in himself and found his purpose through music.

"I started taking piano lessons at age four. I'd just sit there for hours and listen to records, and then sit at the piano and play them. It came naturally to me. I could just learn by ear. I never was into anything else but music. My parents encouraged me to play all I wanted, but when it was time to go to college things changed. They pushed me to study accounting. They worried about my going into the music business. I gave accounting the old college try, but it was not for me. I couldn't do it. I was that kid who was so passionate about music that it was all I wanted to do."

"I talk about this with the *Idol* kids today. I don't encourage anybody to drop out of college like I did. College was not where my heart was, so it didn't make sense. If you're not sure if you want to be in music or be a lawyer, then you should be a lawyer. You have to be that passionate about music, because it is so demanding. I want to hear an Idol kid say to me: 'I can't do anything but music. It's all I want out of life'."

"I did whatever it took. I moved to New York. Just by accident, I was in a piano bar and lucky for me the piano player didn't show up. I sat in and left with 40 bucks after a half hour of playing and thought, this is it. I worked in piano bars for five years, practically seven nights a week. It was there that I met all the girls and guys who were on Broadway. I learned every pop song ever written. It was a great training ground."

"I was hired to be a rehearsal pianist for Barry Manilow. Two of the people who worked for him were part of the team for season one of *American Idol*. They called me one day and said, 'You know every song ever written and we want you for this new show. It's last-minute but can you come in tomorrow and audition?' As crazy as it sounds, I told them that I couldn't, because a friend of mine had asked me to her house for a luncheon. I didn't want to disappoint my friend and I hadn't even heard of *American Idol*, so I told them, 'no'. When I told them I couldn't make it, I didn't think much of it. I had no idea that the show had really taken off. I went to the lunch and later told my friend 'I got a call from *American Idol*', and my friend started to scream, 'call now' so loud my hearing went out. I made the call and started three weeks later."

"The best part of my job is seeing these amazing kids coming in when they are so green, and being a part of that transformation. The relationship between the pianist and the singer is about as intimate as you can get. These contestants are under so much pressure. We're off on Sundays, but the kids are going seven days a week. There's not a break for them and for the lucky ten, it's a big meal ticket and a fast pass to show business. And they know it. I create my room as the safe place. They can sing a bad song, hit a bad note, be dressed hideously, have a breakdown and cry. It's OK."

"Music matters to me because . . . music can change people's lives and I love that. I know it sounds corny but it really is true. There are very few things that can do that for people. Music is one of those things."

Chapter Fifty-One: Simon Perry

Simon Perry could be called the ultimate music manager. As the Chief Creative Officer and Head of A & R for ReverbNation, he makes sure that all of the support pieces connect together to help the 3.8 million musicians, labels, venues, and industry professionals do their thing. ReverbNation's motto is "Artists First". Technologies like "gig finder", "tune widgets", and "promote it", enable users to streamline and manage their content. Simon is also a writer and producer in his own right. He understands the product, having written as well as co-produced the multi-million selling mega-hit album for Chris Lee, the winner of Chinese Idol. ReverbNation began in 2006 in North Carolina, and now employs over 100 people in Durham and New York. The company also started a charity in 2013 called Music for Good. *Triangle Business Journal* named ReverbNation as one of the best places to work in 2012, 2013, and 2014.

"I grew up in England and I have been a music fan my whole life. My big brothers and sisters were huge music fans and so there was always music playing in the house. I remember, from the time I was as young as six years old, I would watch *Top of the Pops* on TV, a popular British music show. I'd then stay up late trying to learn the words to as many of the greatest hits I'd heard that night. I have always felt a connection to music, and that is why I love working for ReverbNation. It was created to provide an opportunity for artists to connect with their fans. I work with great people every day and get to help the best independent artists be heard above all the noise on the Internet."

"There are so many components that artists need to manage in today's music world. For example, they need to distribute their music, connect with their fans, market their music, and promote their shows. ReverbNation provides artists with technological tools like 'promote it', an online marketing tool. We give them a place to control all these pieces

215

from one dashboard, so the artists can organize and manage the assets of their career. This allows them more time to focus on creating their music."

"The slogan 'Artists First' means that we value them. In a world where artists and fans can be directly connected, instead of putting industry first, we believe that the artists can be in the driver's seat to build their careers. I think that this approach appeals to artists. A highlight for us was when we hit the three-million-artists mark and became the biggest market in that space. I also think that the speed with which the company has grown has been exciting. We were named one of the 500 fastest-growing companies in the country in 2014 by *Inc. Magazine*. Curation, talent identification, and putting it in a user-friendly package provide the foundation for what we do. But we didn't stop there."

"In 2013, one of the founders and company president, Jed Carlson, felt that while initiatives like Live Aid were great platforms to create awareness around social issues and causes, these events primarily catered to the big marquis artists. He believed that the large number of developing artists represented a huge number of fans between them and could be just as powerful in their own way. This is ReverbNation's contribution to the idea that fans can be a powerful voice advocating for important causes around the world. Every artist chooses a charity to support and half of the proceeds go to the charity and half to the artist. When a fan buys a song from a ReverbNation artist, it is a way to show support not only for indie music but for a worthy cause. We have around 12 charities and over 116,000 artists in the program. It is a win-win for the artist, the charity, and the fan."

"Music matters to me because . . . when all is said and done, and everything else dies, the music still lives on."

Chapter Fifty-Two: Jonathan Pieslak

Jonathan Pieslak, an associate professor of music at the City College of New York and Graduate Center CUNY, has pursued a career involving contemporary classical composition and is also a Ph.D. scholar who studies music, war, and radical culture. Jonathan received a Guggenheim Fellowship in 2011 to pursue his research, and will publish a book in 2015, *Radicalism and Music*, which explores music's profound but often overlooked role in a variety of radical cultures, including al-Qa'ida and eco-animals rights militancy.

"The role of music in my life growing up was not particularly significant. I took music lessons on the piano and played a variety of instruments as part of my grade school education. We had music in our home, but I never seriously considered being a musician. Neither of my parents were musicians, nor was anyone in my family a professional musician. It was not until I was a teenager that I became interested in music. My interest was largely kindled through MTV, and it was in my teenage years of the late 1980s when MTV really established itself as the primary music television broadcaster. It exposed me to a large number of different bands, and I wanted to rock 'n' roll. I learned the electric bass and played in just about anything that needed a bass player."

"Recently, my scholarly interest in music involves an exploration of the art form's power in violent circumstances, focusing primarily on the influence of music used among American soldiers and Marines during the Iraq War. I saw how music helped ease homesickness, bonded soldiers, and motivated them before combat. The next stage that I have taken in my research has branched off from that study and is a comparative survey of music in radical cultures, specifically al-Qa'ida, racist skinheads, Christian-affiliated extremism and militant animal-rights activists. I am currently finishing a book on how music operates within those varying radical cultures, exploring the profound similarities among uses of music within these different radical groups."

"One observes a great deal of consistency in how music operates, whether intentionally or not, in the processes of improvement, social bonding, membership, and motivation for action. What stands out particularly is the idea of creating in-group and out-group, 'us versus them' mentality, and an over-simplification of victimization. There is also a constant call to defend something. For instance, if you look at jihadi propaganda, there is a glorification of martyrdom, and constant calls for a defense of the ummah, the general Muslim community. One can find similar messages in the militant animal rights movement, with an uncompromising call for the defense of animal rights. The messages themselves are remarkably similar, and the process in which music is used to infill hateful attitudes, has a great deal of parallelism among those groups."

"I really did not have great expectations about what I was going to find. I was not even aware that, in fact, some of these radical cultures were as musical as they were. For example, there is a Straight Edge movement that promotes abstinence and compassion for animals but expresses these feelings very aggressively in music. It was not until I really started digging into that moral mindset that I began to understand the role of music there."

"For a scholarly audience and particularly those interested in terrorism and political violence, I hope that my work provides a greater understanding of the role of culture within radical groups. Normally, the topic of culture does not prominently make its way into discussions of radical groups. From my research, however, it became very apparent that often times the cultural aspects that operate in important ways in these groups, like music, facilitate coercion. And the history of American radical groups has constantly shown that those lacking a flourishing culture of music often do not generate the momentum to have significant longevity."

"Music matters to me because . . . of its appeal to my emotions. It is an exceptionally powerful art form, often times reaching and impacting people's behaviors and attitudes in ways that they might not fully understand. My hope is that we can better understand this impact, avoiding the tendencies towards violence that are articulated by radical groups through their propagandistic uses of music."

Chapter Fifty-Three: Joe Rey

As a director and production designer, Joe Rey's résumé reads like a who's who of top corporations and artists: Chrysler, The Backstreet Boys, Dr. Pepper, LeAnn Rimes, and Busta Ryhmes. Growing up in Camden, New Jersey, music was always playing in the neighborhood. Joe honed his technical skills with some of the best directors in the business such as Martin Scorsese, Jonathan Demme, Terry Gilliam, Hype Williams, Marcus Nispel, Bob Giraldi, and Joseph Khan. Some of Joe Rey's production designs have been honored as part of a permanent collection at the Museum of Modern Art. Joe's ever-expanding creativity finds him on the cusp of a new adventure, a science he has coined, called POPOLOGY®.

"I pretty much grew up on listening to the radio. Before I was born, my mom was part of the first group of dancers on *American Bandstand*, a show that began in Philadelphia from 1955 through 1959. Music was very much introduced during my childhood because my Mom loved to dance. Radio dance music was an important genre for me in the 1970s and 1980s. I loved to listen to Madonna, and Michael Jackson; really, all kinds of music. As I got older I turned to more rock 'n' roll music. I think that early exposure to music made me want to be a part of music video creation, and being involved in the filming industry was the direction I took."

"I went to the Art Institute in Philadelphia for a couple of semesters. Actually I went until the money ran out. We were a very low-income family, and my mom had to spend my tuition money for living expenses. I had to drop out when I was 16. Not having a full education, per se, it makes a young mind anxious, so I became a 'professional intern' to learn the skill of film-making. The production company that I was working for put me with director Garrett Brown. He invented the Steadicam and won

222

Oscars for it by using it in *The Shining* and *Rocky*, and lots of other classic movies."

"As I learned more about production design and art I thought I could fill a niche. I printed out $40 worth of business cards and called myself a production designer. I started getting gigs pretty much right away. It was basically good old-fashioned tenacity. In the late 1980s I hooked up with a friend who was building a film studio in Philadelphia. At that time, Philadelphia was becoming the market film town. Stuart Levy hired me to be his assistant to help him build Metropolis Studios. I pitched Stuart on the idea of me having my own shop attached to the film studio and he went for it."

"In late 1989 we opened Metropolis Studios as a premium & premiere shooting stage within the Philadelphia city limits. We were getting top-run commercials and features accomplished. Then we got into music videos. I went to New York to pitch our studio. I remember this one company called Classic Concepts Production Company that headlined a director named Lionel C. Martin, an important member of the music video world. I convinced Lionel to hire us. Well, the first job that he called us for was the unknown band called Boyz II Men. We did 'Motown Philly', and then a few weeks later, the video was on MTV, blowing up."

"After that experience, Lionel C. Martin became a substantial client for me, bringing Bobby Brown, TLC, Keith Sweat, Lavert, Whitney Houston, and many more. My road to directing was supported by a lot of talented directors that taught me. From each experience I learned something and built on it. I started to work with other production designers, like Hype Williams. This was in early 1991 when no one was really rapping. I started doing rap music videos that included Busta

Rhymes. This escalated to working with legendary artists like Janet
Jackson, Spice Girls, Mary J., Dr. Dre, The Offspring, Joan Osbourne, and
many of the early greats of the 1990s."

"I then went into my own business called ACME Art Department,
(Art Department for Commercials Music Videos, Etc.). We had a bi-
coastal art team that would basically do all the work from New York,
Philadelphia, and L.A. I went on to build VH1's sound studio in 1994 /
1995. The sets had to be really cool, big, elaborate, Techtronic, and
interesting. It was very competitive work. I also did work for MTV. When
MTV was branding itself and expanding into Asia, they sent me as a
production designer. I got to work on *Austin Powers*. I co-directed with
Joseph Kahn working on Backstreet Boys' 'Larger than Life', and I got to
design the many spacecraft sets, and shoot B-Camera."

"I've had so many amazing opportunities, because if I worked one
good job, then I got the next. In one sitting, I couldn't even tell you all the
projects and artistries that I have been a part of. I can say that from the age
of 19 to pretty much age 36, I worked relentlessly, full-time."

"But, in 2001, two weeks before September 11, I had my Jerry
McGuire moment. It was a cathartic experience of questioning myself. I
asked, 'What is MY message? Who am I in this business? What more can
I contribute?' That is when I came up with this word POPOLOGY®. It
was built on all the pop culture experiences I'd had up to that point."

"Then September 11th happened and I thought, 'We need a peace
strategy, some form of creative production that is not political, that
endorses and supports brands, and promotes music and religion and grief
systems through the science of popular culture'. It took me 14 years to get

here. It is about getting people to join in the conversation about the science of what is popular. I believe that the concept of what is popular needs to be shared. I want people have an equal voice with corporations and media advertising. I want to create awareness."

"My question is: are you participating, or are you a passive consumer? Pop culture can actually take more from you than you are putting in. I don't want popular culture running people. I want them to have the tools to direct it. We are basically creating a media literacy education curriculum with POPOLOGY®. We are creating micro-licensing opportunities where you can pick your favorite music videos, and then tell your story of why you love them, (al 'a D.I.Y. MTV) which basically gives more airplay to those videos. And it's your own assessment of what is popular. You can create your own station. You get to be the program director and you can put out media you want people to know about. It's a combination YouTube-Spotify environment on legal steroids."

"Music matters to me because . . . I matter to music!"

Chapter Fifty-Four: Marc Ross

Rock the Earth grew from a concert at the base of Mt. Shasta. This perfect natural setting combined with music inspired Marc Ross, an environmental attorney, to combine his two passions: protecting the environment and music. He formed an organization that does positive work in a unique way. Rock the Earth has worked with over 500 bands to inspire activists to defend the environment at over 1200 concerts since 2004, making a difference through music.

"Music was always in my life. Neither of my parents were musicians, per se, but both of them loved music. I went to concerts at a very early age. I remember listening to Harry Chapin, Peter, Paul & Mary, the Kingston Trio, and there were always The Beatles and Bob Dylan playing when I was growing up. Music was just a part of my life from a young age. During my adolescent years, music became a refuge and salvation for those trying times during adolescence when you don't always see eye to eye with your parents. Music was an escape, and a release."

"I decided to form Rock the Earth in 2002. I was (still am) an environmental attorney who used to go to a lot of concerts (still do) with other environmental professionals and activists, and we would sit around at the show, or after the show, and talk about environmental issues. We realized that there was this gap, where you had lots of artists and fans who cared about the environment, but no organization to represent them. There were groups that occasionally got rock star spokespeople to help them out, but there was really no group that represented the musicians and their fans on important environmental issues. As fans ourselves, we knew musicians had issues that they would like someone to take up."

"The inspiration came to me, to provide a service to the musicians and their fans by harnessing the power and the exposure that musicians have, and utilizing this to accomplish great things for the environment. As an environmental advocacy organization, we work with the music community, fans and bands, to protect some of the world's most threatened places. We have a very accomplished legal and technical team that works on the issues, while we have dozens upon dozens of committed, involved volunteers. These volunteers attend concerts and festivals to conduct environmental education, outreach, and citizen activation."

"Music is a great vehicle to help support causes. Musical artists have a huge platform and a huge audience of people that they tap into emotionally on a daily basis. Artists who are willing and able to allow themselves to use their art and their audience to inspire people to take action on environmental issues makes for a pretty powerful force. We aim to take the issues that the musicians care about, educate their fans about those issues and get them inspired to take action."

"There have been a number of highlights for us, which are what make this job rewarding. The biggest highlights have been the victories in court and on the environmental issues themselves, leading to protection of some of the world's most threatened places. Another satisfying highlight is when artists like Jack Johnson or Bonnie Raitt have given us money to work on particular issues. There have also been opportunities for us to play a major part in the environmental programs at music festivals such as Bonnaroo and Summer Camp. That has been quite an achievement. There is also the fact that we've recruited over 10,000 people over the last 10 years to become members of Rock the Earth, and have had over 50,000 join our mailing list. This tells me that people are pretty excited about Rock the Earth and what we do. The last thing I am pretty proud of, in terms of achievements, is that we have worked with some of the biggest (and most varied) names in rock 'n' roll: everyone from Dave Matthews, and Tom Petty and the Heartbreakers, to The Vans Warped Tour, Journey, Ozzie Osbourne, and Bon Jovi. Some of these music partners we approached because we felt that they care about environmental issues, or that they have a demographic that we really want to hit. But sometimes they just call us, like Bon Jovi's people did."

"Music matters to me because . . . it can inspire action that changes the world."

Chapter Fifty-Five: Valorie Salimpoor

Photo Credit: Peter Finnie

Valorie Salimpoor studies the brain and music. From an early age she was drawn to ask questions. Why is the sky blue? Why do we feel emotions? Why is chocolate good? As she tells the story, a song inspired her to pursue training in the sciences. She found her career path after receiving a B.S.in Psychology/Neuroscience from the University of Toronto. She went on to get an M.S. in Clinical Psychology (Developmental) from York University, and a Ph.D. in Psychology/Behavioral Neuroscience from McGill University. Her postdoctoral fellowship at the Roman Research Institute, Baycrest Hospital, allows her to study why we find music so pleasurable.

"Music has always been very important to me. Growing up, I played the piano, the violin, and the guitar. I had great music teachers and I liked music so much, that I would try to figure out how to play each song I was learning on all of my instruments. I was also interested in the brain and how it functioned. I wanted to discover why people felt different emotions. I wondered why some people like chocolate, and others get addicted to drugs or gambling. My interest in music became a central focus for me as I grew up. I wanted to know why we enjoy music and why it gives us pleasure."

"One day, soon after I had graduated with my neurosciences degree, I was in the car listening to music. I was feeling a bit low because I was still trying to figure out what I wanted to do with my life. I had two degrees but I wasn't sure where I wanted to take my learning. Brahm's "Hungarian Dance No. 5" came on the radio, and within seconds I went from feeling down to feeling elated. I wasn't sure what had happened, but I was aware it all happened in my head. Nothing happened outside of the car. I just heard sound organized in a particular way, and somehow the sounds changed my mood and how I was feeling. I thought, this is really cool and

231

this is what I should study."

"I went straight home and Googled 'music in the brain', which eventually lead me to Dr. Robert Zatorre's lab at the Montreal Neurological Institute where I completed my Ph.D. We started a series of experiments to figure out why music is pleasurable to the brain. We used sophisticated brain imaging to see what happens to your brain when you listen to music you really like."

"For a recent study, we asked people to bring in music that gave them chills and music that they found pleasurable. We had them listen to this inside the brain scanner. We found that when they experienced the peak moments of pleasure, they were releasing a chemical called dopamine in certain parts of the brain. Music can produce a significant increase in dopamine in the nucleus accumbens, which is a part of the brain that is involved in forming expectations."

"When people are listening to music that they have heard before, it activates the nucleus accumbens in anticipation of something good. When you listen to music and the first few notes of your favorite song come on, you get very excited because you know the rest of the parts you like are coming up. If the music gets cut off, you get annoyed. This anticipation plays a big role on how we appreciate music."

"This is important, because the part of the brain that reinforces good biological behaviors, like eating and sex, also works with music. It's incredible that the pleasure experienced to music targets the same areas as addictive drugs. In fact, you often hear people say when they're listening to music that they love that they are experiencing a rush. But unlike drugs, music does this naturally. It's fascinating."

232

"The second area of the brain, called the superior temporal gyrus, is also involved in the experience of music. The genres of music that a person listens to over a lifetime impacts how the superior temporal gyrus is formed. The superior temporal gyrus alone doesn't predict whether a person likes a given piece of music, but it's involved in storing all the music you have heard in the past. It makes a difference as to how you listen to music, and each of us listens to music differently depending on the exposure we have had with the style and genre. For instance, a person who has heard jazz before is more likely to appreciate a piece of jazz music than someone with less experience with that type of music."

"The brain works somewhat like a music recommendation system. Music is a great brain exercise. You are preparing your brain for quick thinking. You are getting exercise with visual, motor, and spatial skills. Listening or playing music allows for practicing all of that for better learning in the future."

"Music matters to me because . . . it makes me feel good."

Chapter Fifty-Six: Matt Sanchez

In 2007, Matt Sanchez, along with Zac Barnett, Dave Rubin, and James Shelley formed the band that would be known as American Authors by 2012. Through hard work, and tremendous talent, the band's rise from jobless to record deal reads like a classic nineteenth-century American "rags-to-riches" tale. In 2013, American Authors' song "Believer" won the Overall Grand Prize in the 18th Annual USA Songwriting Competition. In 2014, their other top hit, "Best Day of My Life", was ranked by Billboard's chart of Adult Pop Songs number one. In 2014 Billboard Top New Artists list ranked the group number nine. With a national tour opening for OneRepublic, and numerous TV appearances including *The Macy's Thanksgiving Day Parade, Good Morning America,* and *Conan,* American Authors is infusing the world with their engaging brand of positive music.

"Music played a big role in my life growing up. In fact, it was always playing in our house. I took to the drums instantly because I loved being able to create my own rhythm. Music offered me a way of bonding. It was a way for me to relate to other people, and it was a way to express myself no matter what I felt."

"For Zac, James, and Dave, music was an important part of their lives growing up, as well. We all started playing music very young. The dream of becoming professional musicians was always something that each of us just knew we wanted to do. When we met each other as a collective at the Berklee College of Music and formed the band, we instantly clicked. We knew that we wanted to do this for the rest of our lives."

"The band just came together easily perhaps because of our deep connection to music growing up and having the same dream. Zac and James met in the songwriting club at Berklee when Zac was president. Zac and I had been playing in previous projects together, and Dave found us when he messaged Zac on Facebook one day, asking him if he wanted to write music or just play music together. We needed a bass player so Zac hit him up and he's been with us ever since."

"We chose the name 'American Authors' because we all tell stories through our lyrics. If you really listen to our songs, they're mainly just observations or experiences we've had both individually and collectively. Also, since I'm from Texas, Zac is from Minnesota, Dave is from New Jersey, and James is from Florida, we each bring our distinct experiences and backgrounds from across the U.S. to our group."

"Our story of struggle is such a positive one and I think it speaks to our music as a whole. Before we were signed we all were basically jobless. Hurricane Sandy had just hit and parts of New York were destroyed. The city seemed like it was in shambles. I remember at one point there was a black-out in the city and there was such a feeling of worry. It was all just crazy during that time. We were deeply affected by everything that was happening around us and interestingly enough this is where our song 'Believer' stems from. That is the song that started everything for us."

"Traveling the world and playing in historic venues like Red Rocks, Ocesa in Mexico City and New Year's Eve in Time Square has been a dream come true. We really are living out our dreams. What's not to love about meeting and connecting with your fans from all over the world? We are some of the luckiest people, and we are so grateful for the opportunity to make music together."

"Music matters to me because . . . it's my waking thought and sleeping dream. It's my way of life."

Chapter Fifty-Seven: Kim Seiniger

For Kim Seiniger, music has always been in her life in one form or another. Whether it was as a member of the orchestra in high school or working as one of the first mobile DJs in the country in the 1970s, music has provided a common thread in her life. After graduating from Colby-Sawyer College with a business degree, she set her sights on being a part of the music industry in Los Angeles. In 1987, she joined Paramount Pictures in the music department and worked her way up to become Executive Director of Music Production. She is celebrating her 28th year at Paramount.

"Music was something that I always loved growing up. I played violin in the orchestra in high school, and then when we moved and I changed high schools, I learned baritone horn. I grew up during the time of disco in the 1970s. I started DJ-ing as my summer job right out of high school. It was really fun. I actually became one of the very first mobile DJs in the country. At the time they didn't even have mixers or anything like that. I had to have mine built for me. I worked in the Hamptons and did private parties and taught people how to do The Hustle."

"It was during my high school years that I knew what I really wanted to do was to become a record producer. But coming out of college, I learned that there was no such job out there. You can't just go get one. So after I graduated from college, I decided I wanted to go to California to pursue a career in music. First I went to San Francisco and there really were only two companies there that did music production. It was quite hard as a female to get a job in a recording studio because it was a very male-oriented business. I actually ended up becoming a security guard at Chevron Corporation for a while."

"I was still determined to be in the music business, and knew I needed to go to Los Angeles. One day I just got in my car and moved down to L.A. I ended up getting a job in the mailroom at Casa Blanca Records in about 1978. When Polygram Records bought the company out we all lost our jobs, but I found a way to stay connected to studio work. I worked as an assistant for a producer named Brooks Arthur. After that I did a couple of engineering jobs. And then something really strange happened that helped my career."

"I was in between jobs when the United States government enacted a requirement that, in order to be employed in this country, you had to show them that you were an American citizen. Everybody had to fill out the I-9 form. There was a temp job in the Paramount music department for somebody to go around to all the musicians Paramount had ever hired with a little Xerox machine. The job was to have them fill out this I-9 form to prove that they were allowed to work in this country. I got that temp job and that's how I got into Paramount. Now here I am 28 years later, doing music production, which is what I have always loved to do."

"I am one of the people who is in charge of all physical recording at Paramount. We are in charge of pre-production and production, which means getting music on the set so people can move to it, or dance to it, or play a band to it. And then, of course, the biggest part of our job is post-production."

"Music comes in lots of different forms in motion pictures. For example, you have a main title song, the underscore of which is usually orchestral. You also have source music which is a piece of music that comes up for a few minutes – say the actors are driving in a car and they turn the radio on – and then, you have licensed music, and you always

240

have end-title credit music. When we get a script, the first thing we do is go through it to see if there is any music mentioned in the script."

"If we get a script and an actor sings, for example, 'She can drive my car' and I know that is a line from a Beatles' song, we have to make sure that line is cleared. Another thing that a lot of people don't realize is that, say they show a scene of a room that has some album covers on the walls, those have to be cleared also. Basically, any time you say a recognizable thing, or even hum something, or you see a recognizable thing, it all has to be cleared and we have to pay for it. Believe it or not, even the song 'Happy Birthday' is not free."

"But we also add music to film if needed. Maybe there is a scene where the actors are talking to each other, but in the background you see a band on stage playing a rock song. We have to consider if that is going to be a live band playing on the stage or if they'll record it on set. Or are we going to have musicians who pretend they are playing and then we bring the music in post-production? I am also one of the people who is in charge of making sure we have somebody there playing active music on the set, or to make sure that the actor gets to the vocal coach if he or she needs to sing something."

"Music, to me, supports all the emotion of a motion picture. No matter what aspect of film you are looking at, you have to have music. For me, music makes the picture really come alive. In post-production, that is when we will go in and score. I have to set up all the studio sessions. I hire the contractors to hire the musicians. I hire any engineers. I get all the equipment set up and delivered there. I actually go to the session."

"I love working with the artists. I work with the best musicians in the world and the greatest artists. The best part of my job is that I get to stand there and watch a 100-piece orchestra play a score. It is just incredible to watch the musicians sit there and read the music perfectly. Most scoring is done in Los Angeles because the musicians here are just phenomenal. They get it done so fast. This is all they do. It is incredible."

"I am also one of the people in charge of payroll for everybody afterwards, and making sure all the union contracts are correct. After everything is done, we usually do a soundtrack album for our movies, and I do all the label copying and the credits on the soundtrack album."

"The job is really diverse. To be in the music department at a major studio is pretty fun. I don't have a glamour job. I have a 'nuts and bolts' job. I don't get to go to the Grammy Awards and the Academy Awards like the big boss does, because I am a production person. I am not the head of the music department, but I would not have been here for 28 years if I did not love it."

"One big highlight has been being in the studio and seeing some incredibly famous artists perform, like Carole King, Barbara Streisand, Michael Jackson, Justin Bieber, Katy Perry, and Pharrell Williams. I remember one day I was in the studio, sitting down watching the orchestra, and this guy was sitting next to me in a plain white T-shirt and jeans and had these dark glasses on. I looked over and thought, 'Wow, that's Jack Nicholson'. I called my mom and said, 'I've been sitting next to Jack Nicholson all day!' We also have little performances here in our office. I think it was two years ago that Imagine Dragons came by and did a lunch performance for us."

"It is really fun to be part of that excitement. Of course just being around the studio lot is really cool. The other day there was a llama roaming around because they were shooting something with a llama in it. Sometimes there's an elephant on set, or the *Glee* cast is prancing around. Sometimes I don't know if things are real or not. For example, there might be some cops walking by here and I wonder, 'Are those real LAPD?', but then the cop turns out to be Angie Harmon!"

"Music matters to me because . . . it is a universal connection for people on all levels. There is no race. There is no discrimination. Everybody is touched by music."

Chapter Fifty-Eight: Whitney Showler

Music for Relief was founded by the band Linkin Park in response to the 2004 Indian Ocean tsunami. Music for Relief has raised over $7 million for survivors of multiple disasters across four continents, since forming in 2005. Music for Relief responds to disasters accelerated by environmental causes like Hurricane Katrina, or other disasters like the earthquakes in China, Haiti, and Japan, or the cholera outbreak in Zimbabwe, or the Ebola disaster in West Africa. As Chief Operating Officer, Whitney Showler organizes benefit concerts, online auctions, and many other activities to help people in need around the globe.

"Music played a very important role in my life growing up because I was a dancer. I listened to music all the time. Music and dance helped me express what I was feeling and get through the tough times. It also motivated me throughout my life. I played piano when I was in grade school, but I stopped at about junior high to focus on my dancing. I often wish I had stayed with it."

"I was working with the band Linkin Park in another capacity, doing marketing for their record label, Machine Shop Recordings, when I began volunteering for Music for Relief. I was very interested in the work that they were doing to provide global humanitarian aid following natural disasters, and so I asked if I could volunteer some of my time and lend some ideas to the organization. Not long after that, I took on a greater role and I am now running the day-to-day operations of the organization."

"I think there are many different ways that music can help ease suffering. Music is a way that people across cultures, across experiences, and across the world can have an emotional connection, and can share with one another what it means to be human and to have hope. Listening to or creating music often helps people feel better regardless of their circumstance. At the very least it helps people connect with one another. At Music for Relief, I have seen music help so many people; specifically when artists have donated songs or lent their voices to help support our humanitarian work, we raise more funds and the awareness for our programs. Not to mention the music fans who rally together by following the lead of their favorite artist. It is inspiring for me to see how music fans step up and help others."

"It is incredibly moving to travel to communities where Music for Relief has worked. There are so many success stories that have stuck with me after my visits. The first would probably be Haiti following the 2010 earthquake. I got to see communities of people who unfortunately are still living in internally displaced refugee camps even though it has been several years since the devastation. Obviously that is not the best of circumstances, but to see people who are moving on with their lives, to see their courage, and their perseverance is extraordinary. The same is true about my visit to Japan after the 2011 earthquake and tsunami. I was able to meet young children who were using music to help process their feelings about the tragedy they had experienced. I saw the dignity with which they faced that disaster, and its aftermath. I am fortunate to have a unique perspective through my job. This makes me understand what people are capable of."

"Music matters to me because . . . it changes lives."

Chapter Fifty-Nine: Sydney Sierota

Photo Credit: Nicole Nodland

Growing up in Southern California with three brothers in a musical household made it easy to form a family band called Echosmith, in 2009. Little did these siblings know that, by 2013 they'd be named one of the 100 Bands to Know by Alternative Press, and, in 2014, recognized as an MTV Artist to Watch. They have appeared on *Conan* and MTV's hit series *Awkward*. Sydney's voice has been described as "stunning", and though she is getting attention, she remains as grounded and laid-back as the warm California sunshine.

"Music surrounded us growing up. There were always musicians, songwriters, and artists, coming to the house. Somebody was either listening to music or playing it. Music was a huge part of all of our lives. We did not really know much of anything else, so forming a band seemed natural to us. Music was really in the family already. We loved the idea of how a blacksmith shapes metals. As musicians, we are shaping sounds, and Echosmith was the first name that we all really liked. So we went for it."

"We really love the early '80s new-wave music, like Joy Division. We also like Fleetwood Mac, The Killers, U2, and those bands. We combine these different sounds and we make it our own, but you can definitely hear the influences. We prioritize writing about life, from our perspective, in our songs. We say what we feel, and not what we think we should say just to sell records. We stand for honesty in our music. We hope people hear the positivity in our album. We want people to be really excited about life like we are, and express it."

"Two of our songs share that message. We have a song called 'Talking Dreams' on the album. This song actually only took us two hours to write, and then we got in the rehearsal space and played the perfect beat for it the first time. It came together so naturally and easily. This song shares our perspective on life. The first line is, 'This is a short race; this is a short life'. We hope it inspires people to go for their dreams. We don't know how long we are going to be here, so let's try to be our best while we can. The second song, 'Cool Kids', is about a boy and a girl who just want to fit in and be cool. I think all of us have felt like an outsider at some point. In this song our message is that being yourself is cool. You don't have to try to be like anybody else, because what's the point? There is already that person in the world. You don't need to try to be like them. It is a reminder for all of us that we do not need to try to conform."

"I would not be who I am without music. Music breaks down barriers and it makes room for conversation. Music opens up so many opportunities to share. It hits the spot like nothing else ever will. When we hear that our music is helping people, it reminds us why we are doing this. I love hearing stories about how the music we write connects with people. It is really encouraging to hear stories like that. Many people are hurting right now and music really does help to heal."

"Music matters to me because . . . of the special connection and interaction it creates, that you cannot find anywhere else."

Chapter Sixty: Beau Silver

Beau Silver's musical talents secured him a music scholarship from the University of Miami, where he graduated with a degree in music engineering. His musical background and software engineering skills made him a sought-after employee in Silicon Valley. Beau's older brother, Jay, set out to transform the world with MaKey MaKey, as co-inventor of the Makey Makey Project. Makey Makey turns any object into a touchpad. Beau used MaKey MaKey in his Stanford University Masters' final project for Computer Research in Music and Acoustics. Next step: the bananama-phone. This musical instrument elaborately combines the MaKey MaKey with bananas. Using alligator clips and electricity to create circuits, Beau effectively demonstrates that music is what you make of it.

"We here at Makey Makey believe that anyone can be an inventor. We like the idea of repurposing everyday objects. MaKey MaKey allows you to manipulate an object's expected purpose. In general, a banana is something you eat, but if you were able to repurpose it to give it a new meaning, then a banana could be an instrument. If you start to repurpose other things, like a plant or a fork or a book, then you start to see the world differently; instead of as it is, you see it changed to the way you'd like it to be. It's really empowering."

"MaKey MaKey lets you transform everyday objects into computer interfaces. It's a USB device that plugs into your computer. This allows you to make your own switches. One way I like to describe MaKey MaKey is that you can press the keys on the keyboard, but you're using something else as the electronic resister in the circuit. Maybe it's a banana!"

"I use MaKey MaKey to create new musical instruments. I created the bananama-phone in my final project for my electronic music course at

Stanford University. It's a totally unique instrument. Think about the piano as an example. There are many rules because of the history about how it should be played and how it should sound. When you build your own instrument, like a bananama-phone, there are no rules. You might be able to play it with your toes or your head, or fast or slow. I want you to make up the rules."

"Music has always been a creative outlet for me. Music makes me happy in the world. I took marching band and choir through high school. I would have had a much harder time in high school if I hadn't had that creative outlet. I play in a band now, so music is a huge part of my life. I believe music can act as a creative outlet for everybody, to help them be more productive and focused. People think there's a division between music and math, between the arts and the sciences. But with theory, acoustics and tuning, and figuring out how different notes harmonize with each other, it makes music just as mathematical as calculus. Music is just as important as math, and yet music programs continue to be underfunded because people don't believe that music can be as practical as math and science programs. MaKey MaKey is a perfect example of how these areas come together. It's an educational, creative, and unique way to explore music."

"Music matters to me because . . . I believe that sound vibrations are the essence of life. Yoga is my spiritual practice, and there's the belief that everything is vibrating. I believe that music is, in a way, the essence of life."

Chapter Sixty-One: Gene Simmons

Rock and Roll Music Hall of Fame, KISS; Gene Simmons's résumé is rich with accomplishments that include singer, songwriter, actor, and entrepreneur. His ability to reinvent himself while still staying true to his persona enabled him to build and continue his successful career. His story is well-known. Born is Israel in 1949, he moved to New York in the mid-1950s with his mother. They had barely enough to get by, and these early experiences had a profound effect on him. Music has always been a part of who he is and who he imagined himself to be.

"When I first heard music I couldn't speak a word of English. I connected to the music through sound and beat. These sounds were like something I'd never heard before. My taste was for rock and roll: Chubby Checkers, Elvis Presley, and The Beatles. I thought the sounds were great. So even before I knew English, I could appreciate music. Then when I started to understand the words, music actually meant something to me. That started happening in 1959, at the birth of rock and roll."

"It's fascinating to me that all the people you look up to, like Led Zeppelin, The Beatles, The Rolling Stones, Jimi Hendrix: they didn't go to school to learn how to play. They taught themselves."

"I was the same. I started singing in a band before I learned how to play an instrument. Then it became clear to me that I should pick up an instrument so that I could increase my chances of being part of a band. Even though I could play a little guitar, I picked up the bass, because I noticed everyone wanted to play the guitar and there were fewer bass players. I knew if I could play bass, I was increasing my chances of getting in with a band."

"When you're young, you don't have the experience and perspective to make smart decisions. You haven't had any life lessons. I knew that music keeps you off the streets. The streets are the enemy. That's where all the aimless guys spend their time. These are the guys you are going to end up rubbing shoulders with unless you stay off the streets. Music is a great way to get your mind wrapped around something exciting. Music has no limitations, and it became my life."

"Once upon a time, music was the rallying cry of youth. It was anti-war or anti-establishment. Whether that was misguided or not, that's not the point, because music was the rallying cry for the culture. Now there's no culture of music. It's just pop. It's background stuff. You go to a club and you listen to music, but there is no sense of 'we', of nationhood."

"Of course, today it helps to be playing rock and roll, or a version of it, because it's popular. If I was just knee-slapping and singing, 'Michael, row your boat ashore, hallelujah', that kind of goofy country stuff, it just wouldn't connect with people. By playing the right kind of thing on electric instruments, singing lyrics that people like and then putting on a big show, all of it helps. But at the end of the day if you could really point to one thing that makes someone successful, then we could all repeat it and do exactly that same thing. Some of it is having the right thing. Some of it is being at the right place, and then, of course being there at the right time, but it's different for every person. What matters to me, is that during those two hours that you see us play, you forget about the traffic jam or the argument that you had with your girlfriend. If that is the only thing that happens, then we've succeeded."

"Music matters to me because . . . if it weren't for music I wouldn't be here. I wouldn't be doing all this stuff. Music unlocked the keys of what's possible and what I can dream."

Chapter Sixty-Two: Eric Singer

Photo Credit: Charlene Bidula

Growing up in Connecticut, music and engineering fascinated Eric Singer at an early age. He fell in love with the saxophone, an uncommon instrument choice for a child. But he excelled at it, and by high school, was playing professionally. Eric attended Carnegie Mellon University, earning a degree in computer engineering. He studied music at the Berklee College of Music and computer science at New York University, receiving an MS. With his gifted talent in both music and computers, he thought it was a natural progression to make musical robots. A leader in robotics who has been called "one of the world's foremost robotics artists", Eric created the League of Electronic Musical Urban Robots, or LEMUR.

"Music played an enormous role in my life growing up. By the age of 10 I was playing tenor sax, and by high school I was playing professional gigs. I started out playing jazz, mostly bebop and in big bands. In college, I formed a rock band, and through the 1990s, I played in dozens of Ska bands. Being a musician and an engineer, I combined these interests as early as high school, and more formally, throughout my college career. By 2000, I had created many unusual, human-playable, electronic musical instruments, and felt like it was time to move forward. In my mind, musical robots are the flip side of the coin – instead of the electronic controls going into a computer, they come out and go to musical robots. Very few people were working in the field at the time, and I felt I could build a group around this idea. LEMUR began from that inspiration point."

"We do many things with robotics. We create as well as modify instruments. For the computer piece, I start with a standard computer interface called MIDI. It's like a USB port, but designed specifically to make electronic music. Any musician who works with a computer or synth knows it and can use it. MIDI notes, whether written by a musician or composed with the aid of a computer, are sent electronically to a microprocessor computer on a chip. The microprocessor translates MIDI into electrical signals to control motors and other devices that play notes on physical instruments. By using MIDI, and putting the 'smarts' on the microprocessor, the musician does not need to know the deep technical details of the instruments – he or she can just compose and play. As for the physical side of designing and creating the instruments that make the sound, I had to learn and teach myself mechanical engineering, machining, and robotics, skills I didn't possess when starting LEMUR."

"The LEMURtron is a large collection of instruments, which go into an interactive installation. My favorite single instrument is definitely the GuitarBot. It's the first robot I built. It has since been updated to version two, and is an 'electronic slide guitar-like instrument' with independent control over each of the four strings. The instrument can play its own part or follow a musician in perfect synch. It's better seen in person or at least on video than described, but for over a decade, there was nothing like it in the world. Now, I'm starting to see instruments on the net that are inspired by it. The instruments are agnostic to music type and have been used to play in styles such as bluegrass, Indonesian music, jazz, avant-garde, and rock, as with They Might Be Giants. Also, others and I frequently use computers to compose and improvise on the instruments, often aided by the interaction of people seeing them in installation."

"To see the instruments used in as many contexts and by as many musicians as possible, is very gratifying and inspiring for me. This is why we've done everything from creating installations, to producing concerts, to being commissioned to make robotic instruments for others. Highlights have included installations at The Smithsonian and many other museums, performing with some of New York's top contemporary and 'downtown'

258

musicians, and building our magnum opus, an 'orchestrion' for Pat Metheny, which toured the world for a year."

"I hope people take away that these are real, serious instruments, and are meant to augment what musicians and composers do. They are yet another way of making music, like every instrument: from the violin, to the electric guitar, to the synthesizer, to the musical robot. I am always thinking of ways to combine art and technology, whether in the form of musical robots or projects involving other media."

"I will often look around my environment, see something, and ask myself, 'How can I make this into a musical instrument?' A rubber tube, a Slinky, and some homemade 'slime' were the inspirations for the Sonic Banana, the Slink-o-tron, and the Slime-o-tron, respectively."

"Music matters to me because . . . of its dramatic importance in my life, though I don't feel I can answer this question in a way that gives it justice. It would take an entire book."

Chapter Sixty-Three: Dan Storper

Just outside of New York, in a town called Great Neck, on Long Island, a young Dan Storper could be found listening to the limitless variety of 1950s and 1960s music. Harry Belafonte, Sergio Mendes & Brasil '66, the Four Tops, the Spinners, and Ray Charles all found their way into Dan's musical education. Dan took piano lessons, and listening to the music greats captivated him. Those early songs stayed with him, and in 1993, Dan created Putumayo World Music to introduce people to the music of the world's cultures. The label grew out of his Putumayo clothing company, founded in 1975. Celebrating its 20th year, Putumayo World Music is considered a pioneer in selling world music to the non-traditional market. The company's slogan, "Guaranteed to make you feel good", came from the fabric of American radio and those very sounds Dan grew up with.

"Putumayo evolved out of a series of fortunate coincidences. I was returning from a trip to Indonesia and stopped in San Francisco to see an art exhibit being carried by a friend of mine. Walking through Golden Gate Park on my way to the exhibit, I saw Kotoja, an African band that was performing there. They combined pop melodies with an African beat, and I was really struck by them."

"Three days later I stopped into one of my stores and they were playing thrash metal music. I felt that was inappropriate for an international retail shop that sold Latin American, African, and Asian handicrafts and clothing. It made me want to put a soundtrack together. I wanted the music to reflect the places that I had traveled to, and that was appropriate to the culture of the stores I had created. I made a mix with some world artists and some of my favorite American artists like Bonnie Raitt, Van Morrison, and Bob Dylan."

"The music was very well-received. Customers kept asking about it and where they could purchase it. Like with any great idea, one thing just led to another. I had the good fortune of already having sold the Putumayo clothes and handicrafts to many American retailers, so when I started putting the music collection together, I'd built in a natural audience. I approached a friend who owned a record label and asked him about doing a compilation of world music. That's what really led me into this career."

"The CDs took off, even though the industry has gone through so much turmoil and so many record stores have closed. I think that our model is sustainable because one of the more unusual and important things that we do is sell to gift shops, museum stores, bookstores, cafés, and children's stores. We figured out a really great way to connect with people, because they are hearing our music in a non-threatening environment. It bypasses the need to get a radio hit or a television hit, which is really hard to come by these days."

"I think there are very few things that really connect people. Music, food, and sports are all things people enjoy, regardless of where they are from. So whether it's a great song, a delicious meal, or a wonderful game of soccer, these things basically are representative of a culture, and they connect you with the positive side of that culture. What I hope is that people fall in love with a style of music, an individual song, or an artist, and then they become more curious about those places, which is wonderful. World music inspires curiosity and interest. It adds some emotional bonding with these cultures, which is why the experiences are so unique."

"Music matters to me because . . . it makes me feel good and it's what I do."

Chapter Sixty-Four: Morgan Taylor

Art and music played an important role in Morgan Taylor's life growing up. The youngest of three, his older siblings' musical repertoire permeated the house. Morgan found an early comfort in playing and doodling to sounds. Music and art became a necessary part of his life, and he held music-related jobs from everything to sound engineer to rock musician, sharing the stage with Bob Dylan to Wilco. Gustafer Yellowgold, Morgan's childlike creation from the sun, who finds a home in the coolness of the Minnesota countryside, was a product of his upbringing, steeped in music and art. Morgan has created award-winning music videos and toured nationally with his multi-media shows built around Gustafer Yellowgold. His inspiring message is aimed at kids and adults: slow down and appreciate the wonders around us.

"I was the youngest of three kids and there was a pretty big age gap between all of us. My sister is 12-1/2 years older than me, and my brother is seven years older. When I was born, they were old enough to be interested in buying music. There was quite a big record collection in the house. Music was really important. I felt like I always wanted to have a record on when I was playing, and so I would put on a record. I didn't really know what the songs were about, but I got a feeling from the songs and then I would sort of act out what I was hearing in the music. That became a really important part of my education growing up."

"When I moved to New York City from Dayton, Ohio, I completely overhauled everything that I knew. I felt like I found my creative voice in New York. I had the option of starting another band, but I just couldn't stomach it. I thought, there has to be something more exciting than this. That's when my wife suggested I explore my art and music project. I had always kept the two separate."

264

"I realized that I had written and accumulated all these playful story-songs, which were sung in first person, that I was not playing in my band. I didn't know who the voice would be for these songs until I started to illustrate. As I started drawing them out in the form of a picture book, using some cartoon characters that I had developed over the years, I realized there was a whole world. I drew two songs' worth of pictures and bound them into a little book."

"When it came time to draw the front cover of the book and to name this guy, I kind of pulled the name out of the air. The name Gustafer sounds funny and friendly, Yellowgold is descriptive, and put together it makes the whole thing sort of a tongue-twister. Gustafer Yellowgold combines many turns and twists just in those syllables. Before I knew it, I had him. The reaction to Gustafer was immediately positive. Right away it felt like it was something that I wanted to pursue. I needed to see just how far I could take it."

"I take my craft very seriously. I love humor, especially the kind of humor that takes you by surprise. I wanted to incorporate that into my art. We were blessed by that very original *New York Times* quote that described my production as 'Dr. Seuss meets Yellow Submarine'. This gave me a bar to try to live up to for inspiration; and while there is never going to be another Dr. Seuss or Beatles, it is a pretty inspiring combination of entertainment elements to try to live up to."

"I provide a music and art multimedia experience. I sing and play the songs next to a giant movie screen, with my animated illustrations in a moving storybook form to correspond with the music. It's for all ages, but for me the challenge is to engage the adults. I don't want it to be something that the adults are just tolerating. I want people to get absorbed

265

into the world of Gustafer. Music allowed me to find my true creative voice. It allowed me to find myself. It provided the opportunities to travel and play that I was not getting before. That has been the greatest thing."

"Music matters to me because . . . there is no other feeling like it. It's a way to be drawn out of your own thoughts and get sucked into someone else's experience."

Chapter Sixty-Five: Chris Vance

Chris Vance was drawn to music at an early age. Every format interested him. He loved listening to his mother play the accordion and the piano, hearing the choir sing in church, relaxing with music video games, and losing himself by simply turning on the car radio. Music played such an important role in his life that he dreamed about making music accessible for everyone. That idea started Chris on his creative journey. In 2010, while working as a marketing executive for Bartle Bogle Hegarty, one of the world's most famous creative advertising agencies, Chris founded Playground Sessions. The app is a 21st-century piano teacher. Chris recruited YouTube piano sensation David Sides to help him develop the popular music video instruction library. This nontraditional, innovative way to learn music became an instant hit.

"I like video games. I wanted to know why Guitar Hero and Rock Band were so popular and inspiring. I realized that people are instinctively drawn to these video games because there's a strong calling inside all of us to express ourselves musically. We don't want to just be passive listeners. We want to actively participate in the creation of music. It just dawned on me one day that the traditional way of learning an instrument doesn't work for everyone. Private lessons are unaffordable for many, and people often don't have the access to instruments. I had this crazy idea to make Guitar Hero and Rock Band but with real instruments. My hope was to have people continue to play the real instrument, because there is so much positivity and emotion that's evoked from playing a real instrument instead of a video game."

"Playground Sessions addresses areas that we felt were shortcomings in traditional learning. We created a library of music that you hear on the radio, that you sing and dance to, and appreciate so that you want to play it. One of the great things about Playground Sessions is that you can choose the music that is familiar to you. This means that it is easier to learn because you already know the song so well."

"The other piece that we wanted to create was personal feedback, because one of the benefits of a private teacher is that you get comments from your teacher. We were able to use groundbreaking technology to give students that instant response. The keyboard is connected to your computer, and if you play a note right or wrong you immediately know, because it turns green if it's right, and it turns red if not."

"We were inspired by video games and the ability to pick and play music that you really loved. But we wanted to offer more. We included the elements of gaming with merchandise stores, awards, leader boards, and progress reports. These incentives keep you engaged and motivated, so you continue to practice and learn."

"Also, music by its very nature is social. People learn by sharing and collaborating. Part of enjoying music is sharing your expression of it with others. We wanted students to be able to share those musical expressions. We incorporated a social feature as well. I think whenever you are playing music you are connecting emotionally. Music gives you a creative outlet. Music facilitates how you develop emotionally. It's a way for kids, in particular, to express themselves. Not all kids are great about communicating, but they can express themselves musically, which is in itself a form of communication."

"Music matters to me because . . . without it I'd be lost."

Chapter Sixty-Six: Gus Van Sant

The constant scores of Sinatra playing in the house provided a perfect backdrop for Gus Van Sant's pursuit of art. The Oscar-nominated director found his passion early, with film being the strongest, but he also dabbled in painting, photography, and music. As a child, he moved often, attending high school on both coasts. This allowed for an infusion of the West's mellowness and the East's avant-garde. He attended Rhode Island School of Design, where he locked into cinematography. He is known for making bold societal statements in his films *Milk*, *Drugstore Cowboy*, *Last Days*, and *Good Will Hunting*. His work reflects a considered searching from big budget to intimate indie film-making. A central theme of his is finding one's place in the world.

"I was always drawn to art. I remember when I was in junior high school my art teacher really inspired me. He would paint in class, the same as Robert Levine, and so I started painting – I think because he made it very interesting. I just kept painting and realized how much I liked it. At every school I attended, I was always in the art department."

"I had another teacher who showed us experimental films that combined cinema with art. This genre came out of the New York experimental cinema, because many New York filmmakers who were making experimental films were also painters. I started doing similar things, like drawing on film and so forth. Later when I went to high school, I made a sound film with another student for my senior project. It was a 16mm sound film, which, when we started, we had no idea how to do. But we got it together and figured it out. It was in that film that I incorporated music for the first time. I then went on to art school."

"I think that my art experience allows me to be very organic as a director. Each story that I tell is different, so the approach is pretty much

271

changed for each film. I really just begin. Even if I have set plans before starting, there are things that happen during the filming process that I want to incorporate as I work, which changes the original plan. I tend to be very organic. I really do not set too much of a structure just because so many things can happen in the process. I like to take advantage of those unplanned events."

"The one area where I like to have a set framework is with the music. I think for me and probably for most filmmakers, music has some kind of relationship to the story. A great many filmmakers, depending on the kind of music they like, are very into it – to the point where sometimes they are composing a score or deciding on music before they shoot. I always have an idea of what music I might like before we shoot. I know that it can change during the shoot, so I don't get too set on it; but there is an idea. After I have film footage, I'll have the music put to the film footage to see what it's like. The way that music fits into a given scene or a shot is pretty immediate. You see right away whether or not it works. I usually discover this in the editing process. I often try out different types of music in a scene."

"I'm interested in taking a different approach to film. Right now, I find the films made by these young German guys from JuBaFilms very inspiring. They use dance to tell a story. I don't even know if they are out of high school yet, but they are producing these films and they are pretty cool. It's not slick like a music video."

"When I was making music videos, I realized that it was a difficult process for me. I'm not really good at that type of thing, so I stopped doing them. I did make different recordings on my own, as well as some records. This was the result of finding a recorder that was a multi-track recorder in 1980 when I was working in New York. I bought it mostly to make soundtracks for my films, in order to mix sound to the films, but then it became very apparent that I could not record music. It was kind of a hobby to make these finished songs that exist somewhere in the world, but it stayed as a hobby."

"Music matters to me because . . . it adds emotion in films."

Chapter Sixty-Seven: Dave Wakeling

Dave Wakeling believes in giving. He grew up in England as part of the working class during the 1950s and 1960s. This was a time of great political, social, and musical transformation and upheaval. In 1979, Dave formed The Beat, also known as The English Beat in the United States. What started much like *The Little Engine That Could*, a few working class kids espousing a positive message of peace and unity, tolerance and acceptance, quickly became a phenomenal hit. Dave would tour with all the greats: The Clash, David Bowie, The Police, REM, The Pretenders, and The Talking Heads. Despite his worldwide popularity, however, Dave never wavered in his vision. He gave back to causes that meant something to him, such as nuclear disarmament. While his signature teardrop guitar sits in the Rock and Roll Hall of Fame, Dave's attitude about fame remains firmly-grounded.

"When I was growing up, music did not play an important part in my life until one emotional night. I was a competitive swimmer. If I won a medal, my dad would buy me an orange soda to drink, and I got to listen to the car radio on the way home. One night I won a handful of medals and was very excited and emotional. I had the radio on and I heard, 'Don't Walk Away Renee' by The Four Tops, and 'Ruby Tuesday' by The Rolling Stones, and I still swear to this day that I was not crying; that it was the chlorine from the pool. But tears were just flooding down my face and my whole body felt electric. It was something that happened at that time which transformed me. The excitement and the adrenaline that I felt in swimming, I started to feel in music as well, only it was stronger. My dream to become a musician began that night, but the dream was so big I thought it would never happen. I thought it would always remain just a dream."

"My dream began to become reality when I was living in an

apartment and I was writings songs and singing them. The people living there would say 'That's a good one', and 'Oh, I like that one!' I joined a 1950s revival band for stage experience, and then convinced Andy Cox, my school friend and writing partner, to join a lounge cabaret group. He wore tuxedos and I wore leather pants and sang, 'Chantilly Lace'. After a few weeks of working with others, we were dying to start our own group!"

"In 1978 we formed The Beat. The group stood for many things. On the one hand it stood for enticing, uplifting beats in music. On the other hand it also stood for stark and introspective lyrics about the nature of the human life and love. Touring with the band was a stunning whirlwind for me. I have exciting memories of famous musicians, like sharing an elevator ride with David Byrne and David Bowie."

"I also remember going down to the phone booth box at the corner of the street on a Tuesday morning at 9:00 a.m., to phone the record company to see what the number of my record was in the chart. Sometimes I was walking back really happy with a newspaper and a cigarette. What's odd about it is that the emotional aspect of the experience is so strong, that you really cannot cope with the enormity of it all. You just act like you know what's going on, and appear blasé, to deal with the pressure."

"About seven years ago, I decided that this was the right time to bring back The Beat. The Beat still stands for the same things. I think life is a tragedy, but it is also beautiful, and you have the best of times when you remember both of them at the same time. So you're not really sad and you're not just riotously happy for no reason; you are a bit of both. We have been on tour, evolving and changing the lineup. We have some new songs, and we play the old songs, and people like it. Our new record,

'Here We Go Love' will be out soon, and then we will be on tour with it. We like to play music that opens people's hearts and hips. Hopefully then the lyrics and the ambiance open, stimulate, and comfort all those who come to watch us and hear us play."

"I have analyzed my songwriting and there seems to be something of a process. First, there is a sudden flash of inspiration, and then anywhere from about two weeks to nine months of work. The first verse of my song is to lay down my personal feelings about something that touched me: a story, state of the world, state of mankind, state of my heart, whatever inspires me at the time. The first verse is personal and somewhat confessional. The second verse tends to be the examples of that sort of theme that you've observed in people's lives, to try to make a connection. The third verse attempts to come to some kind of conclusion: where does that put us, and where do we go from here? Part of it is self-exploration. Then you are back to the chorus."

"In terms of songwriting, it seems to me that there has been a bit of a Renaissance. The technology that is used in music now has changed it to the point where you can't really tell the difference between instruments like you could before. It's allowed the composing part of music to go through the roof, and everybody's got the ability to be his or her own orchestra."

"There is less mass-marketing of music today, and the major labels do not have the strangle hold over the whole scene. There are small boutique operations and lots of people coming up with creative ways to try to utilize and maximize the modern social media as a marketing tool. Some of it shows fascinating options for the future."

"Music matters to me . . . because it makes me feel good, and because I see it as Carl Jung's theory of mass consciousness most positively executed."

Chapter Sixty-Eight: Narada Michael Walden

Photo Credit: Bill Reitzel

Born in Kalamazoo, Michigan, a small country town where they make Gibson guitars and Kellogg's Corn Flakes, Narada Michael Walden was destined to play the drums. While the sparkling colors of the Mardi Gras drum set initially attracted him, it was the complex sound of the instrument that fascinated him and held his interest. At the age of nine, he began lessons, and his natural talent became quickly apparent. He could use both hands, both feet, and sing simultaneously. Narada has an Emmy and is a multiple-Grammy-Award-winner. He has produced and written songs for some of the all-time greats like Whitney Houston, Stevie Wonder, and Mariah Carey, but he is a musician first and foremost.

"My childhood was brilliant in the sense that music was around me all the time. My dad wasn't a drummer, but he loved drumming, so there was always music in the house. I'd watch records spin for hours. I'd play on pots and pans and boxes and pie tins. The weather was never very good. The snow and rain out there kept me inside. You have to find something to do, and music was that thing for me."

"When I was 10, I saw Stevie Wonder play at the Regal Theater in Chicago. He was playing harmonica and drums and the girls were screaming. I remember thinking, 'Wow! This is really exciting when you can play music like that and have people scream in pure ecstasy. It's unbelievable'."

"I wanted to play music so beautifully it would inspire people. I worked hard, and when I was just 20, I got my big break. I went from being a busboy at Mario's Place, a restaurant in Connecticut, to recording an album with The Beatles' producer, Sir George Martin, in London Air studios. Music has connected me with some of the most famous people in the world. I'm proud and honored to have worked with some of the greatest. Gladys Knight, Aretha Franklin, George Michael, Elton John, Sting, Whitney Houston, and Mariah Carey are just a few highlights."

"When I play, it takes all of me. I'm using more of my power, using more of my spirit, using more of my heart, using more of my physicality. I believe that it's God's grace that allows me to do what I do. I told God, 'If you give me the opportunity to play music I won't forget you. I'll stay grateful'. And I do. I stay grateful. I want to represent everything good. Music is a balancer. I believe that everyone comes onto this planet to do good things. When it's all said and done, I don't think God cares about whether you had a good time. I want to be able to say, 'I did a great job. Lord, I rocked and rolled and sweated. I got people to sing and clap and rock and roll and spin down the aisles and go crazy'."

"Music is magic. I don't know anything that is so powerful, that can make people so happy, and excited. Without music, kids are suffering and violence is on the rise. Kids need to be busy doing music. It is something that takes their full concentration, so then they don't get involved with things that aren't good for them. I think music saved my generation."

"Music matters to me because . . . it's my only mission on the earth. Music matters to me because without it, I'm nothing on this earth. Music is essential to me."

Chapter Sixty-Nine: Liv Warfield

Liv Warfield grew up with a musical dream. She had a beautiful, soulful voice and a desire to become a star. The trip from Peoria, to being part of Prince's The New Power Generation, has been nothing short of magical. She has been described as "Prince's muse" and "Prince's protégé", and named VH1 Soul's "You Oughta Know" promo-campaign 2014-featured artist. She also produces her own unique brand of music. She is multi-talented.

"I was always around music as a child. I grew up in a gospel church, so I got gospel in my blood. I also began playing violin starting around the age of six. I played through my freshman year in high school. My ears were always ringing with music growing up."

"I knew I wanted to be some kind of performer and entertainer, but was really too scared to let my family, or anybody, know that I could sing. I kept that hidden. When I moved out to Portland and lived on my own, I felt a sense of freedom. I was able to do and try anything musically. A friend of mine told me about a bar where you could get up and actually sing in front of people. I couldn't believe it. She told me it was called 'Karaoke', and once I tried it, I was hooked. It introduced me to another world of music, and I was so excited. I was in that Karaoke bar maybe six times a week, from 8:00 until 4:00 in the morning. I was there constantly. I discovered Karaoke and my voice."

"People told me that I had talent, and encouraged me to put up some YouTube clips. That's where Prince found me. It's really remarkable that he saw me on a YouTube clip. A friend of mine told me to send Prince a video. I remember responding, 'Send my video, for what? That's a long shot in the dark'. I could sing in front of 50 people, but that is a long way from singing in stadiums. My friend sent in a clip anyway. I didn't hear

283

anything for three or four months. Then I got a call and everything in my life just changed. Everything was frozen in time when I got that call. It obviously changed my life forever."

"Singing with Prince on the same microphone is indescribable. It's a trip to be that close, and to be sharing the mike. These are my 'all time' moments. I can't believe that I get to watch him arrange and conduct the band. I love it, because you can see him working. You can see his mind working. My life's highlights have definitely been being on stage with him."

"I see music as a melting pot of R&B, of jazz; a melting pot of everything. I use my voice to inspire, just as I find my inspiration through my own life story—my struggles, my triumphs. I am inspired by whatever touches the heart. I don't force it. It just comes and hits me. I want to get people in that frame of mind, where they can listen to music and it takes them someplace. It takes away problems. I hope they feel a sense of freedom in an engulfing musical journey."

"Music matters to me because . . . it's freedom."

Chapter Seventy: Taylor John Williams

How do you get from working at a dog hotel in Portland, Oregon to becoming the fifth-place finisher on 2014's *The Voice*, Season 7? The show premiered with almost 13 million viewers. Once Taylor John Williams auditioned and became a member of Gwen Stefani's team, his life went into warp speed. With close to 71,000 followers on Twitter and new material to work with, Taylor is discovering his musical path, one song at a time.

"Music is the one thing that I have that has always come easily to me. It is something I feel like I was born with. I have the ability to hear intricacies that I think not everybody can hear, and I connect with music instantly. I was always singing to music and loved listening to it from an early age. It just kind of happened. I didn't have to seek it out too much."

"I always knew that I had the ability to be a professional musician if I wanted it badly enough. I didn't always know this was what I wanted to do. I was pretty shy as a kid in grade school and high school. I became a bit more introverted from grade school to high school. While it was always a dream of mine to be a professional musician in the back of my mind, I never thought it would happen because I was just too shy. But eventually I developed a love for writing which led to poetry. When I picked up a guitar and discovered that I loved the guitar, I put the poetry and music together and started writing my own songs. I think that's when I really started to develop a desire to have people hear my music and my words."

"I was working at Sniff, a dog hotel, and I played at my work a few times. It wasn't a regular thing. That was added into my story for *The Voice* because it sounded interesting, but it didn't really have an impact on me musically. I was always against the whole reality TV concept,

286

especially when it came to music and competitions. But one day I was inspired to audition for *The Voice*. I thought it would be fun, and a good opportunity to make some music connections. I felt it would be good to do something that scared me and took me out of my comfort zone, so I just decided to go for it."

"I went to L.A. for the open call. For some of the contestants, the show had contacted them specifically, and they got to skip the earlier stages of the audition process. But I started at the very beginning. I did the open call and made it through that first part. There were about three more auditions after that, in front of various people, followed by a lot of testing, and a lot of interviews. They wanted to make sure that the contestants are going to be good on camera. Once that's all done with, and if they love you, they will then give you a blind audition. The blind audition is really like your trial run for the whole thing."

"Being on the show in the beginning was pretty mellow. Not mellow compared to a regular day, but mellow as compared to what happens when you make it further along in the competition. Once you do move further into the competition, it gets pretty intense. But at the beginning, there are a lot of vocal lessons, a lot of wardrobe sessions, and a lot of the details of learning what goes into putting together the actual shows. Once the contestants are whittled down, we had music and practicing every single day. I often had 12-hour days packed with everything you can imagine that needed to be done to prepare for the show. The longer you are in it, the more intense it gets."

"Performing on that stage was very surreal. It's something that I didn't focus on too much, as far as the scope of things, because when you do that it can really freak you out. But after a show I would often just lie in bed and try to fathom the huge number of people that saw me sing on that particular night. If you dwell on that topic of exposure too much when you are in it, you can get too overwhelmed. I became pretty good at numbing myself to that and instead I focused on preparing to perform, as well as performing well at every stage of the competition."

"I think the highlight for me was that the house band for the show is composed of some of the best musicians in the world. That's probably overstating it a little bit, but they really are the best in the business. Being able to walk into the rehearsal room and have a concept of what I wanted with a song and have them just pick it up instantly, and understand the kind of vibe that I was going for, was an amazing experience. They were really fun to work with and very talented. That was probably my favorite part of the whole deal."

"It was cool to be on Gwen Stefani's team. I don't have anything to compare it to because I only got to be on one team, but she was really good about letting me spread my wings and make my own decisions musically. Just being there to maybe offer some advice as far as when I would present to her what I wanted to do; it was a give and take. Initially she showed some reluctance, but once she got what I was trying to do, then 99 % of the time she would just let me do what I wanted. That was really cool. I know that there are other coaches in that season and in past seasons that want to have more of a hands-on approach with their team – which is cool for some people – but I like to do my own thing when it comes to arranging songs and all that. I think for those purposes she was a really good fit for me."

"Being on *The Voice* really taught me a lot. I came in with certain expectations. It's easy to have a preconceived idea about how something is going to be or how you are going to be when you are a part of something like a reality show. I don't know if *The Voice* is just a rare case, but everybody that was a part of the show was so good to me, and to the other contestants. It was amazing. I didn't expect that I would get so much genuine consideration. Given that this is a type of program that runs on a tight time schedule, where everything has to work so quickly and efficiently, you would expect that the people would be a little bit more militant especially with the contestants and with everybody's time. I can think of a few times in the process where I was having a hard time, but I never felt alone. I always felt like there were people in place to take the time and help me deal with those situations. That was surprising for me. I thought I had a clear idea about how it would all work. I figured it would be superficial but then by being on the show I learned that my expectations were not what happened at all. I made a lot of long-lasting relationships."

"Getting back to my music and the real world was at first a bit overwhelming. I was really happy to be home, I had come from knowing exactly what I needed to do for the next week, for the next show, for the next song, where everything is very planned out. Then once I was off the show, I went from having this really clear path and going a million miles an hour to zero pretty quickly. I have been trying to hit the ground running and use this momentum to reach out to people and continue putting music out there. I loved this experience. I know being a professional musician is what I want to do and it's what I am going to do. Now I need to go about making the right moves and being proactive with my music."

"Music matters to me because . . . when I experience things involved with music – with performing it, listening to it, just being around it – I feel indescribable. There are these certain moments where I feel locked into something really big and really broad and something that connects me to the origins of life and meaning. I don't know what that word is, but it's a feeling that is hard to explain. It's something that no other experience has given me."

Final Notes

I'm often asked how this book was written. I interviewed every participant by phone or if he or she preferred, by email. I asked the same questions and transcribed each person's response into a narrative to make the book more conversational. I wanted the reader to feel like he or she was sitting down with the interviewees in person and listening to the stories of their musical ventures and the importance of music in their lives. I always ended the interview with this question: "Please complete this sentence: 'Music matters to me because . . . '." The reflections about music contained in this book continue to inspire me as I hope they will inspire you. Take a minute and ask yourself, "Music matters to me because . . .".

Information for this book was gathered from many sources, including the Internet, personal interviews, and email. All of the interviewees reviewed their individual stories, and had the opportunity to edit them.

The following interviews were conducted by email:

Michael Cartellone

Geert D'hollander

Michael Franti

Christopher "Kiff" Gallagher, Jr.

Bernie Krause

Patrick Laird

Storm Large

David "Lebo" Le Batard

Bibi McGill

June Millington

Matt Sanchez

Eric Singer

Acknowledgements

To each of you who shared your inspiring stories. This book would not have been possible without your generosity and our mutual love of music.

To Ana Ammann: for answering a 13-year-old's email and giving me the opportunity to do what I love. You have always treated me with professionalism and respect. Thank you for supporting and guiding me. I couldn't ask for a better mentor and friend.

To Lynn Robison: for taking that first phone call from a 15-year-old and enthusiastically endorsing my proposal to partner with Fender Music Foundation. You were always available to talk and have taught me so much about the business of nonprofits and the music industry.

To my dedicated publisher, Barbara Terry, and Waldorf Publishing: for believing in my book from our very first conversation. You turned my dream into a reality.

To *Oregon Music News*: for providing me with my first platform and letting me run with it. The idea for this book sprung from my weekly series, "Music on the Street".

To Tom D'Antoni: for teaching me the ropes of good journalism.

To Fender Music Foundation: for welcoming me into the family.

To my English teachers, Nichole Tassoni, Brett Mathes, Virginia King, and Paul Donohoe: for teaching me that "style is how you say what you say" and there can never be too many rewrites.

Music Soothes the Soul   Matthew Bernstein

To my music teachers who helped me find my voice.

To the faculty at The Catlin Gabel School: for fostering my curiosity and creativity.

To my editor, Jahnavi Newsom: who provided invaluable guidance in the writing process.

To Brett Ryder, an amazing artist: who answered my email and allowed me to use his creative image for the book's cover.

To my Uncle Lester, Aunt Heather, and cousins Annabel and Lily: thank you for cheering me on.

To my grandparents who take care of me, encourage me, and support me in everything I do: I know how lucky I am to have you always there for me. I love being neighbors and seeing you every day.

To my parents: for giving me the courage to take a risk, and to my brother, Ryan, for knowing how to make me laugh.

Author Bio

Matthew Bernstein is a high school senior and honors student, with a passion for writing and music. As a staff writer for *Oregon Music News*, Matthew has been conducting interviews since he was in eighth grade. Matthew has written his first book, *Music Soothes the Soul* at the age of 17.

Visit musicsoothesthesoul.com